--- 90 DAYS OF SCRIPTURE ---
LOVE JOY PEACE

Spiritual Growth Journal - Beloved Scripture / Daily Gratitude [SOAP Interactive Devotional Series - 1]

LEE KOWAL ,MDIV

COPYRIGHT

Kingdom Life Books™

90 DAYS OF SCRIPTURE - LOVE JOY PEACE:
SPIRITUAL GROWTH JOURNAL - BELOVED VERSES / DAILY GRATITUDE
[SOAP Interactive Devotional Series - 1]

Send inquiries to: Kingdom Life Books, PO Box 4, Lincoln City, Oregon 97367

Soft Cover Print Edition © Sept 2018 ISBN: 978-1-949261-10-3

Cover Design by *Kingdom Life 365*™, LLC

~

Books in this Series:

90 Days of Scripture - Love Joy Peace

90 Days of Scripture - Spiritual Awarenesses (October 2018)

90 Days of Scripture - God Is… (February 2019)

CONTENTS

SPIRITUAL GROWTH JOURNAL

This journaling devotional relies on God's Word alone to minister & strengthen

The word of God is living and active and sharper than any two-edged sword, and piercing as far as the division of soul and spirit... and able to judge the thoughts and intentions of the heart. Hebrews 4:12 - NAS

~

Scripture speaks for itself — It has the power to change lives! Renew your relationship with God during your private devotional time.

How-to-Journal for Beginners — Prevents Writer's Block with interactive prompts and format.

Teaches How to Journal; 90 days following journaling prompts will develop skills to carry you through years of fruitful devotional times with God & His Word.
Spiritual Growth Themes provide platform for purposeful meditation & prayer.
Daily Focused Bible Verses provide 'touch points' between your spirit and His.
Daily Prayer Summarizes Scripture and serves as journaling prompt.
Daily Praise and Gratitude section to develop a thankful heart.
Challenge yourself to create and personalize your own friendship devotional with God Himself!

Feeding Daily on His Word will intentionally set your mind toward Him for greater intimacy & strength — 90 Days of opportunities for God to draw you by His Love & intimacy!

~

HOW TO GROW SPIRITUALLY USING THIS JOURNAL

Personal private time with God and His Word is exciting! It is important to journal these special occasions so you can look back and be encouraged both by seeing how your personal relationship has progressed, and to be refreshed by reading again how He uplifted your spirit in the past.

In the beginning stages of this journey it may be difficult to get our pen moving across the page. Writer's block can set in and then discouragement follows.

If you do struggle with 'how' to journal in your private devotional time in God's Word, then using this method will help you move forward with your spiritual growth, with a clear idea what to write in your devotional journal.

The interactive SOAP journaling format uses a standard approach to Biblical meditation, reflection, and prayer -- it helps you interact with God's Word and His Spirit.

~

WHAT HAPPENS NEXT?

As you slowly ponder God's living Word, His Spirit works through it to strengthen your spirit in ways that are unimaginable! As you seek Him earnestly, He provides insight, encouragement, discernment, and reminds us of His continuous presence.

You will sense Him lovingly drawing you, you may feel energized and filled with encouragement, strength, and gratitude...This awareness of His presence is only the beginning! As you digest His Word through meditation, your hunger for more of Him will sustain this process in your life! Allow your hunger to be satisfied by His energizing life-giving presence!

~

SOAP JOURNALING EDITION with DAILY GRATITUDE — Helps you to engage with Scripture — Observe/Reflect on it, Apply/React to it, then Pray/Praise/Gratitude! Each day contains Scripture based on a spiritual growth theme. Then a prayer provides a brief summary of the Scripture and serves as journaling prompts for the journaling sections provided See example on opposite page.—>>>

This journal includes interactive journaling sections as follows:
1. Observation / Reflection
2. Application / Reaction / My Next Steps
3. Prayer / Praise / Promises / Daily Gratitude and Thanksgiving

Scripture with Prayer — DAY 63

O God, you are my God; earnestly I seek you; My soul thirsts for you; my flesh faints for you, as in a dry and weary land where there is no water. When I remember you upon my bed, and meditate on you in the watches of the night; For you have been my help, and in the shadow of your wings I will sing for joy. My soul clings to you; your right hand upholds me.
Psalm 63:1,6-8 - ESV

Prayer: Father, it is right and needful that I set my passions and desires upon You alone. It is Your divine purpose and path that will be true joy! Instead of spending time just to be with You, I have pursued my own pleasures and goals, and they have left me empty. Renew my passion to be with You, and enjoy You.

Observation / Reflection

(**Example:** My spirit within can reflect my physical needs by thirsting, and being tired. And As I meditate on God's Word, it nourishes my spirit, similar to how food & water nourish and strengthen my my body, by showing me how God's wonderful power, provision, and protection keeps me safe & secure. His peaceful care will cause me to be filled with joy deep within my spirit.)

Application / Reaction / My Next Steps

(**Example:** Since meditating on God and His Word is so critical for my spiritual vitality & growth, I should carve-out more time in my daily schedule to spend reading and communing with Him. I sense that the little time I have set aside for this purpose has not been enough — My next step is to do a daily 'time-audit' (which activities or commitments I can eliminate), make plans to get to bed earlier, set the alarm to ensure I awaken, etc., I will make plans to set aside time each morning to seek to be with God & His Word.)

Prayer / Praise/ Promises / Gratitude & Thanksgiving

(**Example:** My heart is filled with gratitude and thankfulness that You have revealed just how much I need to be 'consuming' Your Word. Please increase my hunger to read and meditate on Your Word with a healthy spiritual appetite... then, I pray, my passion and desire for You will increase and overshadow everything that once appeared to be a priority over spending time with You! Help me set my heart on the treasure of seeking Your moment-by-moment loving presence in my daily life.)

DIGGING DEEPER INTO THE 'JOURNALING' EXPERIENCE

Each day begins with Scripture and Prayer (prayer summarizes verse and doubles as an additional journaling prompt). follow these steps Daily:

1. OBSERVATION / REFLECTION: Read the Scripture verse slowly and focus on each word to follow the message closely. Read over the prayer provided. ask God's Holy Spirit to help you ponder and meditate upon the Scripture verse(s).

Following the verb actions; what is is saying about what what either Jesus/Father did, or what we should do?

Restate promises, praises, or thanksgivings; if the verse is about a promise of God or psalm of praise/thanks, restate it in a few different ways if possible.

Sit quietly while pondering what you read. While listening to His 'still small voice', record what your spirit is sensing.

2. APPLICATION / REACTION / MY NEXT STEPS: Apply the principle based on your reaction to it. Again, sitting quietly before the Lord, you may see how this particular verse is applicable to your current life situation. Record the 'next steps' you should take in order to develop a more intimate relationship with Him, or fulfill a purpose He has for you.

3. PRAYER / PRAISE / PROMISES / GRATITUDE & THANKSGIVING: Record personal prayer, points to remember, spiritual challenges, personal affirmations or promises that gave you joy and hope. Writing down daily thoughts of thanksgiving and gratitude is a helpful method to direct your mind and heart on the paths of Christ's righteousness — Philippians 4:4-8.

—If time permits, look up the verse provided in order to get a wider context of the verse.

~

OTHER SUGGESTIONS FOR JOURNALING

Record meditation questions and answers, prayers, gratitude, conversations with God. Enjoy reading later the notes you take on your spiritual journey.

Sometimes we cannot remember precious thoughts or perceptions from previous devotions. Spiritual growth can occur slowly, and having previous notes for reference or celebration are helpful, encouraging, and needful.

~

BE INTENTIONAL — Make regular daily time and a place to meet with God.

Opportunity for growing spiritually is always at your fingertips, but you will need to make space and time to slow down, get alone, and purposefully engage God & His Word – to invite Him into your daily life and allow this beautiful transfer of communion and growth to occur!

FOUR THINGS TO DO INTENTIONALLY:

1. Go to a quiet place – *Set a time each day to be alone with Him in solitude.*
2. Read the verses slowly and prayerfully – *Prayerfully seek /ask how to apply it to your life.*
3. Ponder and meditate – Spiritual deep dive, ask questions, seek answers: *After each question, stop and let your spirit sense guidance and direction from God's Holy Spirit. Learn to sense His presence.*
4. Journal your journey — *Observe, Apply, Pray, Praise, Gratitude*

~

Grow closer in relationship to God by seeking Him through His word.

"For everyone who asks, receives; and he who seeks, finds; and to him who knocks, it will be opened." Luke 11:10 - NAS

~

PRAYERFULLY SEEK UNDERSTANDING

Asking yourself questions is critical for spiritual understanding —

Scripture provides a path for your communication with God. Prayerfully ask God to open your eyes to potential adjustments needed to grow closer to Him… He will not withhold truth.

Review the cadence of your daily activities and interactions with people — take note if you observe how the passage may relate to your personal life (including thought-life), or your understanding of God.

A question may be, *"Since joy is promised from our relationship with God I would like to know what that is like. . . What is it I need to change in order to grow closer to God, and experience His great joy and strength?"*

DO I REALLY BELIEVE?

Sometimes the best question is, "Do I really believe this?" —

If you ponder where an unbelief has been buried in 'doing good', it is possible for light to shine in that area and bring growth and strength in Him.

Consider whether there is anything either unseen (spiritual) or seen (unspiritual) that is preventing you from living in full belief of the promises or characteristics of God. Take the steps needed to establish a solid foundation by finding Scripture that will strengthen your faith in that specific area (memorize and meditate upon it).

"For the mind set on the flesh is death, but the mind set on the Spirit is life and peace." Romans 8:6 - NAS

DIG DEEPER

If time permits,

- look up verse reference in Bible and read entire chapter.
- Memorize scripture and take it with you.
- Journal your journey [Daily journaling lines in print version, daily enote place-holders in ebook] & large journaling section every week to capture gratitude, prayers, & conversations with God.

SUBMIT QUICKLY

Quickly submit if you are convicted of any previous misunderstandings of the verse, or if changes are required in your life. Your relationship with God cannot grow if there is unbelief, doubt, worry, or disobedience.

As we submit to & obey Him, He causes our growth. If not, the magnitude of His joy, peace, love, and brilliance of His presence may slip away from your countenance.

Start your journey with a willing & hungry heart! He is always there ready to fill you with His Love.

DON'T GIVE UP!

It is not uncommon for us to commit to following through with a 365 spiritual growth devotional, and then fall behind. Before long we feel so guilty we stop all together.... One thing I have learned over the years, God understands and He is always waiting with open arms!

Please, know that you are not alone. Our enemy Satan would love for you to feel so guilty or discouraged that you stop all together. Do not give in and pray it through!

3rd Millennial life is busy, yet as we grow closer to God we slowly begin to let go of things that no longer bring satisfaction, thus freeing up space for developing a relationship with God. This may not happen over-night.

God never wants you to feel condemned. So be easy on yourself if you are not consistent — Just don't give up!

~

†††

May God Bless You On Your Spiritual Journey!

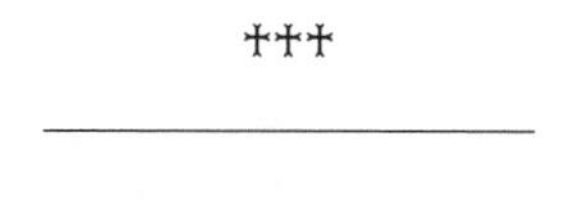

~

WHAT IS SPIRITUAL GROWTH?

I am the True Vine, and My Father is the Vinedresser. Abide in Me, and I in you... he who abides in Me, and I in him, bears much fruit; for without Me you can do nothing. John 15: 1,5

THE GOAL – RELATIONSHIP

Christian spiritual growth is deeply rooted in the Person of God Himself.

Lists of personal attributes and accomplishments *may* be outward evidence of spiritual growth, but these do not ultimately define it. Only those attributes and accomplishments flowing from God Himself, living in our heart, are true signs of spiritual growth. Outwardly they may look the same, but inwardly we are spiritually aware of the difference.

Living a Christ-centered life filled with peace, joy, and eternal fruit is only possible as we abide with Him in relationship.

Since spiritual growth and fruit are not possible apart from this vital continuous connection with Him, intentional effort is required. The degree we purposefully pursue this relationship, to know and be known by Him, is directly related to the quality and magnitude of fruit resulting from these pursuits.

"Apart from Him you can do nothing." — John 15:5

As we slowly become rooted in Him, we begin to recognize this glorious, *incomprehensible, energizing, life-giving* relationship with God is possible!

LIVING & GROWING ON THE VINE

How to live vitally connected to Him. . .

Spend time in His word daily with intention and desire to seek and know Him. After reading the passage, ask Him to show you the truth, ask questions for understanding — meditate upon His word and your relationship grows. You probably won't hear an audible response, but as you sense His Spirit, you will begin to understand *how* He fills your spirit with joy, contentment, and peace. Then as you come to know Him by His presence, you will also sense His guidance.

As you sense Him lovingly drawing you, you may feel energized and filled with encouragement, strength, and gratitude...This awareness of His presence is only the beginning! As you digest His Word through meditation, your hunger for more of Him will sustain this process in your life!

The practice of the Presence of God — It is the schooling of the soul to find its joy in His Divine Companionship

— BROTHER LAWRENCE, 17TH CENTURY

~

Intentionally and daily:
Feast on His Word
Seek Him purposefully
Learn to recognize His presence

~

"Therefore as you have received Christ Jesus the Lord, so walk in Him, having been firmly rooted and now being built up in Him and established in your faith, just as you were instructed, and overflowing with gratitude." Colossians 2:6-7 - NAS

---

†††

LOVE IS . . . (DAYS 1 - 7)

Love is God & He Loves You!

LOVE IS FROM GOD:

Beloved, let us love one another, for love is from God; and everyone who loves is born of God and knows God. 1 John 4:7

LOVE IS OUR NEED:

"The single desire that dominated my search for delight was simply to love and to be loved." — Augustine of Hippo, 4th Century

LOVE IS OUR GOAL:

"Do everything for the Love of God." — Brother Lawrence, 17th Century

LOVE IS OUR PURPOSE:

"Spread love everywhere you go. Let no one ever come to you without leaving happier." — Mother Teresa

PRAYER

Heavenly Father, I come in Jesus name with a heart full of gratitude that You have guided me safely to this point in my life, and have opened my eyes to begin seeking Your love in a fresh new way. I ask that You take me by the hand a guide my feet into the paths of Your righteousness so that I may reflect Your love to those around me. Help me to become evermore aware of Your glorious presence moment by moment, and grow closer to You day by day in vital relationship. In Jesus Name. Amen

Scripture with Prayer — DAY 1

"Teacher, which is the greatest commandment in the Law?" Jesus replied: "Love the Lord your God with all your heart and with all your soul and with all your mind. This is the first and greatest commandment. And the second is like it: Love your neighbor as yourself." MATTHEW 22:36-38 - NIV

PRAYER: Jesus, thank You for showing us the simplicity of Your gospel — to love You and others! Help me see and feel Your love in a great new way. Lord, let my life and my lips tell out the story of Your great love as I experience it myself! I open my heart to receive Your love this day, and seek with all my heart to submit and obey it. Let Your love shine through me to others. Amen.

Observation / Reflection

Application-Reaction / My Next Steps

Prayer / Praise / Promises / Gratitude & Thanksgiving

Scripture with Prayer — DAY 2

LOVE IS SPIRITUAL FRUIT: ***"Sow for yourselves righteousness, reap the fruit of unfailing love."*** HOSEA 10:12 - NIV

LOVE IS ABSENCE OF FEAR: ***"There is no fear in love, but perfect love casts out fear. For fear has to do with punishment, and whoever fears has not been perfected in love."*** 1 JOHN 4:18 - ESV

PRAYER: Father, to sow Your love is to sow living seed… Oh, the wonder of! Let me always sow Your Love instead of fear, anxiety, or selfish ambitions — in peace & joy. I desire to strive for the perfection of You love, to diligently bear Your fruit. Oh Lord, make me a seed sower this day, to scatter Your love wherever I go.

Observation / Reflection

Application-Reaction / Next Steps

Prayer / Praise / Promises / Gratitude & Thanksgiving

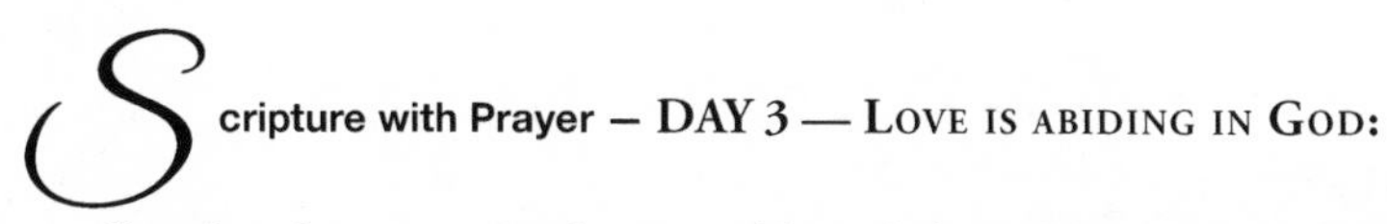

Scripture with Prayer — DAY 3 — Love is abiding in God:

"And we have come to know and have believed the love which God has for us. God is love, and the one who abides in love abides in God, and God abides in him." 1 John 4:16 - NAS

Prayer: Lord, Your invitation to abide in You fills my heart with joy! I long to grow closer to You. Give me grace to eliminate all things that pull me away from You — that I may see clearer Your utter loveliness & beauty, to smell Your sweetness. Fill me.

O*bservation / Reflection*

___

___

___

___

A*pplication-Reaction / Next Steps*

___

___

___

___

P*rayer / Praise / Promises / Gratitude & Thanksgiving*

___

___

___

___

Scripture with Prayer — DAY 4 — YOUR LOVE IS SET UPON WHAT YOU TREASURE:

Do not lay up for yourselves treasures upon earth, where moth and rust destroy, and where thieves break in and steal. But lay up for yourselves treasures in heaven, where neither moth nor rust destroys, and where thieves do not break in or steal; for where your treasure is, there will your heart be also. MATTHEW 6:19-21 - NAS

PRAYER: I ask Father, for wisdom to spend my life wisely, to joyfully focus on heavenly treasures of knowing You and fulfilling Your plan for my life. Your wisdom is eternal and Your Words are life — help my mind & heart focus on them always. Show me how to seek You and find You in the busyness of my life — that my passion is set upon You instead of things that do not truly profit.

Observation / Reflection

____

____

____

____

Application-Reaction / Next Steps

____

____

____

____

Prayer / Praise / Promises / Gratitude & Thanksgiving

____

____

____

____

Scripture with Prayer — DAY 5 — Love Is…

Love endures with patience and serenity, love is kind and thoughtful, and is not jealous or envious; love does not brag and is not proud or arrogant. It is not rude; it is not self-seeking, it is not provoked *[nor overly sensitive and easily angered]****; it does not take into account a wrong endured. It does not rejoice at injustice, but rejoices with the truth*** *[when right and truth prevail]*. 1 Corinthians 13:4-5 - AMP

Prayer: The mystery of Your love surrounds everything, yet it is hidden as a treasure in those who know You. Assist my heart-cry to reveal You through acts of love — to be ever patient & peaceful. Keep agitations far from my spirit, and root-out areas of prideful thinking. Let love rule my life through Your Spirit.

Observation / Reflection

Application-Reaction / Next Steps

Prayer / Praise / Promises / Gratitude & Thanksgiving

Scripture with Prayer — DAY 6

Love bears all things *[regardless of what comes]**,** **believes all things** [looking for the best in each one],* ***hopes all things*** *[remaining steadfast during difficult times]**,** **endures all things** [without weakening]**.** **Love never fails** [it never fades nor ends]. —* ***And now there remain: faith*** *[abiding trust in God and His promises]**,** **hope** [confident expectation of eternal salvation],* ***love*** *[unselfish love for others growing out of God's love for me],* ***these three*** *[the choicest graces]**; but the greatest of these is love.*** 1 CORINTHIANS 13:6-8; 13 - AMP

PRAYER: You have shown me that Your love is steadfast and changeless. Increase my faith, that I truly rely on Your comfort, warmth, and joy — even in sorrows.

Observation / Reflection

___

___

___

___

Application-Reaction / Next Steps

___

___

___

___

Prayer / Praise / Promises / Gratitude & Thanksgiving

___

___

___

___

Scripture with Prayer — DAY 7 — LOVE IS JESUS

Greater love has no one than this, that one lay down his life for his friends. John 15:13 - NAS

Jesus Christ is the same yesterday and today, yes and forever. - Do not be afraid; I am the first and the last. Hebrews 13:8; Revelation 1:17 - NAS

Prayer: Jesus, I can't comprehend Your dying in my place… but in faith I accept Your loving friendship, & rest in Your eternal peace. Help me be a friend to You.

Observation / Reflection

____

____

____

____

Application-Reaction / Next Steps

____

____

____

____

Prayer / Praise / Promises / Gratitude & Thanksgiving

____

____

____

____

GOD'S LOVE (DAYS 8 - 23)

The LORD's lovingkindnesses indeed never cease, For His compassions never fail. They are new every morning; Lam 3:22, 23

~

How precious also are Your thoughts to me, O God! How great is the sum of them! If I should count them, they would be more in number than the sand; When I awake, I am still with You.
Psalm 139:17, 18 - NKJ

Prayer of Apostle Paul:

For this reason, I bow my knees before the Father, from whom every family in heaven and on earth derives its name, that He would grant you, according to the riches of His glory, to be strengthened with power through His Spirit in the inner man; so that Christ may dwell in your hearts through faith; and that you, being rooted and grounded in love, may be able to comprehend with all the saints what is the breadth and length and height and depth, and to know the love of Christ which surpasses knowledge, that you may be filled up to all the fulness of God. Now to Him who is able to do exceeding abundantly beyond all that we ask or think, according to the power that works within us, to Him be the glory in the church and in Christ Jesus to all generations forever and ever. Amen.
Ephesians 3:14-21 - NAS

Scripture with Prayer — DAY 8

I sat down under his shadow with great delight,
and his fruit was sweet to my taste.
He brought me to the banqueting house,
and his banner over me was love.
SONG OF SONGS 2:3, 4 - KJV

Prayer: Heavenly Father, Your love fills me with great delight — my soul sings with mirth! I find all-encompassing warmth and contentment in Your loving arms. I pray that Your Spirit rest upon me as I ponder Your great love for me this day, that my mind and heart be refreshed and strengthened in Your sweetness.

Observation / Reflection

____

____

____

____

Application-Reaction / Next Steps

____

____

____

____

Prayer / Praise / Promises / Gratitude & Thanksgiving

____

____

____

____

Scripture with Prayer — DAY 9 — WE LOVE HIM BECAUSE HE FIRST LOVED US. 1 John 4:19

HE PAID FOR YOU TO BE WITH HIM: ***...you were not redeemed with perishable things like silver or gold from your futile way of life inherited from your forefathers, but with precious blood, as of a lamb unblemished and spotless, the blood of Christ.*** 1 PETER 1:18,19 - NAS

HE IS LOVELY — HE IS YOURS: ***My beloved is mine and I am his.*** SONGS 2:16

PRAYER: As I grow closer to You daily, You continuously reveal the Depth of Your love. Your healing presence gives freedom from guilt & shame — I am free to love. Lord, may I breathe it over & over today, "My beloved is mine & I am His."

Observation / Reflection

Application-Reaction / Next Steps

Prayer / Praise / Promises / Gratitude & Thanksgiving

Scripture with Prayer — DAY 10

Bless the Lord, O my soul, and all that is within me, bless His holy name. Bless the Lord, O my soul, and forget none of His benefits; Who redeems your life from the pit, who crowns you with lovingkindness and compassion; Who satisfies your years with good things, so that your youth is renewed like the eagle. The Lord is compassionate and gracious, slow to anger and abounding in lovingkindness. Psalm 103:1-2,4-5,8 - NAS

Prayer: Oh my Lord, my God, and my King — I bless and honor You with my lips, to bring praises to Your Name! Your immense love & compassion give strength & joy to those who dwell near You. Thank You for Your gracious provision, and eternal life in Christ Jesus. Amen.

Observation / Reflection

____

____

____

____

Application-Reaction / Next Steps

____

____

____

____

Prayer / Praise / Promises / Gratitude & Thanksgiving

____

____

____

____

Scripture with Prayer — DAY 11

"For God so** [greatly] **loved and dearly prized the world, that He** [even] **gave His** [One and] **only begotten Son, so that whoever believes and trusts in Him** [as Savior] **shall not perish, but have eternal life. For God did not send the Son into the world to judge and condemn the world** [that is, to initiate the final judgment of the world]**, but that the world might be saved through Him. JOHN 3:16-17 - AMP

PRAYER: I express my heart-filled thanksgiving to You! I am released from darkness that once ruled my life, to live in Your serenity and peace. Energized by Your Holy presence, I worship and praise You, My Lord & King!

Observation / Reflection

Application-Reaction / Next Steps

Prayer / Praise / Promises / Gratitude & Thanksgiving

Scripture with Prayer — DAY 12

But when the goodness and loving kindness of God our Savior appeared, He saved us, not because of works done by us in righteousness, but according to his own mercy, by the washing of regeneration and renewal of the Holy Spirit, whom he poured out on us richly through Jesus Christ our Savior, so that being justified by his grace we might become heirs according to the hope of eternal life. Titus 3:4-7 - ESV

PRAYER: Saved by Your grace Jesus, my Friend, I stand in wonder that You revealed Yourself to me personally. Your great gift has brought serenity & renewed hope. My heart is filled with gratitude, I am eternally grateful. Guide me this day so I remain close to You, my Savior. Help me keep my eyes on You!

Observation / Reflection

___

___

___

___

Application-Reaction / Next Steps

___

___

___

___

Prayer / Praise / Promises / Gratitude & Thanksgiving

___

___

___

___

Scripture with Prayer — DAY 13 — ***Such hope*** *[in God's promises]* ***never disappoints us, because God's love has been abundantly poured out within our hearts through the Holy Spirit who was given to us. While we were still helpless*** *[powerless to provide for our salvation]*, ***at the right time Christ died*** *[as a substitute]* ***for the ungodly. Now it is an extraordinary thing for one to willingly give his life even for an upright man, though perhaps for a good man*** *[one who is noble and selfless and worthy]* ***someone might even dare to die. But God clearly shows and proves His own love for us, by the fact that while we were still sinners, Christ died for us.*** **Roman 5:5-8 - AMP**

Prayer: My hope in Your salvation from eternal death is strong, grounded in Your love. Father, thank you for opening my eyes to see the my need for Jesus' death and His blood to cover my sins — and my glorious eternal life in You!

Observation / Reflection

___

___

___

___

Application-Reaction / Next Steps

___

___

___

___

Prayer / Praise / Promises / Gratitude & Thanksgiving

___

___

___

___

Scripture with Prayer — DAY 14

But because of his great love for us, God, who is rich in mercy, made us alive with Christ even when we were dead in transgressions— it is by grace you have been saved. And God raised us up with Christ and seated us with him in the heavenly realms in Christ Jesus. Ephesians 2:4-6- NIV

Prayer: Lord Jesus, lover of my soul, In Your grace I am living and seated with You in heavenly places . This new live with You is truly living! Preserve me in a clean heart and rejuvenate me by Your presence. Let me feel Your extreme love, joy, and peace so that I may also share Your true nature with others in my life.

Observation / Reflection

___

___

___

___

Application-Reaction / My Next Steps

___

___

___

___

Prayer / Praise / Promises / Gratitude & Thanksgiving

___

___

___

___

Scripture with Prayer — DAY 15 — ***See how great a love the Father has bestowed upon us, that we should be called children of God; and such we are. For this reason the world does not know us, because it did not know Him.***

Beloved, now we are children of God, and it has not appeared as yet what we will be. We know that when He appears, we will be like Him, because we will see Him just as He is. And everyone who has this hope fixed on Him purifies himself, just as He is pure. 1 John 3:1-3 - NAS

Prayer: Lord, my eyes are fixed on You as a young child! With faith of a child my hope is directed toward living as part of your family — in purity of mind I accept it now, and look toward "what I will be..." in that glorious day of Your Revelation. Bless me with Your abiding presence this day and every day after. Let my every word and act bring glory to Your name.

Observation / Reflection

___

___

___

___

Application-Reaction / Next Steps

___

___

___

___

Prayer / Praise / Promises / Gratitude & Thanksgiving

___

___

___

Scripture with Prayer — DAY 16

Neither height nor depth, nor anything else in all creation, will be able to separate us from the love of God that is in Christ Jesus our Lord. ROMANS 8:39 - NIV

PRAYER: Father of all creation, thank you for loving mankind so much that You gave them a choice to love You back, and for saving me through Jesus. I feel secure & steadfast in Your love — safe from grief, fear & pain. Hide me everlasting God under the shadow of You wings. Show me what behaviors or things I am doing that cause me to wander from Your love, Help me leave them behind, and cleave ever-more closer to You, my loving Savior.

Observation / Reflection

____
____
____
____

Application-Reaction / Next Steps

____
____
____
____

Prayer / Praise / Promises / Gratitude & Thanksgiving

____
____
____
____

Scripture with Prayer — DAY 17

JESUS HIMSELF SHOWED US THE FATHER'S LOVE & COMPASSION

"He who has seen Me has seen the Father." JOHN 14:9

He saw a great multitude, and felt compassion for them, and healed their sick.

MATTHEW 14:14

PRAYER: Jesus, I am filled with peace as I read about Your love, compassion, gentleness, tender-hearted care in Scripture. I stand amazed this same care reveals my Father's dear compassion and mercy for me as well. I ask that You make this even more real to me, so that I see the reality of Your loving compassion in my life, and deep in my heart.

Observation / Reflection

Application-Reaction / My Next Steps

Prayer / Praise / Promises / Gratitude & Thanksgiving

Scripture with Prayer — DAY 18 — *Greater love hath no man than this, that a man lay down his life for his friends. —For the life of the flesh is in the blood, and I have given it to you upon the altar to make atonement for your souls; for it is the blood that makes atonement for the soul.*
JOHN 15:13; LEVITICUS 17:11- KJV

Having canceled out the certificate of debt consisting of legal demands [which were in force] against us and which were hostile to us. And this certificate He has set aside and completely removed by nailing it to the cross.
COLOSSIANS 2:14 - AMPC

PRAYER: Father, Your Word clarified a great mystery — why a blood sacrifice was required to cover my iniquity. Though Your ways are too high for complete understanding, I am eternally grateful to You for saving me from eternal death.

Observation / Reflection

____

____

____

____

Application-Reaction / My Next Steps

____

____

____

____

Prayer / Praise / Promises / Gratitude & Thanksgiving

____

____

____

____

Scripture with Prayer — DAY 19 - THE LOVE OF GOD THRU CHRIST

The Spirit of the Lord God is upon me, because the LORD has anointed me to bring good news to the afflicted; He has sent me to bind up the brokenhearted, to proclaim liberty to captives, And freedom to prisoners; . . .

Giving them a garland instead of ashes, the oil of gladness instead of mourning, the mantle of praise instead of a spirit of fainting. So they will be called oaks of righteousness, The planting of the Lord, that He may be glorified.

ISAIAH 61:1,3 - NAS

PRAYER: Lord, in love You have spread out great blessings for me through Jesus Christ! Help me take hold of Your healing for my heart, and accept Your adornments of gladness, praise, & strength. May Your beauty rest upon me this day and always — to the honor and glory of Your name.

Observation / Reflection

____

____

____

____

Application-Reaction / My Next Steps

____

____

____

____

Prayer / Praise / Promises / Gratitude & Thanksgiving

____

____

____

____

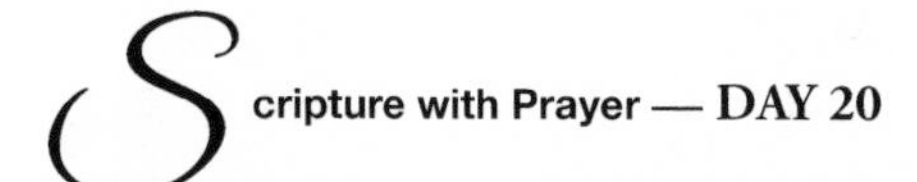

Scripture with Prayer — DAY 20

Bless the Lord, O my soul, and all that is within me, bless His holy name. —Who redeems your life from the pit, Who crowns you with lovingkindness and compassion; Who satisfies your years with good things, so that your youth is renewed like the eagle. — The Lord is compassionate and gracious, slow to anger and abounding in loving-kindness. Psalm 103:1,4-5,8 - NAS

Prayer: Lord, I learn of Your great love and compassion in Your Word and a desire to praise and thank You raises in my heart. Help me to bless You, oh Lord. Let me serve You so that my life, my every step, is a praise to Your glory.

Observation / Reflection

Application-Reaction / My Next Steps

Prayer / Praise / Promises / Gratitude & Thanksgiving

Scripture with Prayer — DAY 21

Behold! The Lamb of God who takes away the sin of the world! — Jesus said, "It is finished." With that, he bowed his head and gave up his spirit… by one sacrifice he has made perfect forever those who are being made holy.

JOHN 1:29,19:30; HEBREWS 10:14 - NIV

PRAYER: Jesus my loving Savior, Holy Pure Lamb of God, it is so wonderful to be alive in You —Thank You for being my sacrifice unto salvation, and for drawing me with Your love! Living now in the fullness of Your extreme joy & peace, I cannot imagine my life without You. Help me walk in Your perfect ways so that my life will draw other to Your loving arms and eternal life.

Observation / Reflection

____

____

____

____

Application-Reaction / My Next Steps

____

____

____

____

Prayer / Praise / Promises / Gratitude & Thanksgiving

____

____

____

____

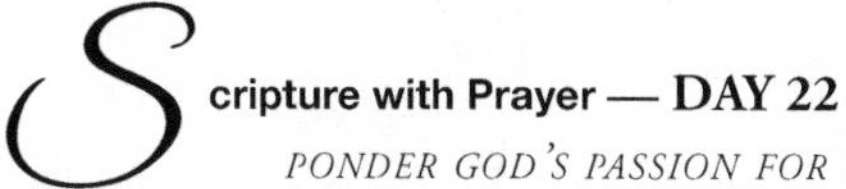

Scripture with Prayer — DAY 22

PONDER GOD'S PASSION FOR YOU, YOU ARE BEAUTIFUL IN HIS EYES!

My dove in the clefts of the rock,
in the hiding places on the mountainside,
show me your face, let me hear your voice;
for your voice is sweet, and your face is lovely.
SONGS 2:14

PRAYER: Oh Heavenly Father, I am amazed that You love me so deeply! I am comforted to know You long to see my face and hear my voice. Grace me with Your powerful loving presence today I pray and keep me ever close to You.

Observation / Reflection

____
____
____
____

Application-Reaction / My Next Steps

____
____
____
____

Prayer / Praise / Promises / Gratitude & Thanksgiving

____
____
____
____

Scripture with Prayer — DAY 23

The Lord is full of compassion and mercy.
— As a father has compassion on his children, so the LORD has compassion on those who fear him. JAMES 5:11; PSALM 103:13
— Jesus Christ is the same yesterday and today and forever.
HEBREWS 13:8 - NIV

PRAYER: Oh Jesus my loving Friend, Your Word affirms to me what I feel from You in my Spirit — I can trust that Your love for me will never fail nor cease — what comfort my Lord. Help me this day, to take each step in thankful awareness of Your merciful presence, looking forward to eternal life in glory!

Observation / Reflection

____

____

____

____

Application-Reaction / My Next Steps

____

____

____

____

Prayer / Praise / Promises / Gratitude & Thanksgiving

____

____

____

____

LOVE ONE ANOTHER (DAY 24 - 33)

They will know we are Christ's followers by our love

"Whatever a person may be like, we must still love them because we love God."

— JOHN CALVIN

"A Christian should always remember that the value of his good works is not based on their number and excellence, but on the love of God that prompts him to do these things."

— JOHN OF THE CROSS

"Constant kindness can accomplish much. As the sun makes ice melt, kindness causes misunderstanding, mistrust, and hostility to evaporate."

— ALBERT SCHWEITZER

PRAYER

Heavenly Father, Cleanse my heart of all ill will toward those I encounter during my daily life. Help me to walk in the purity of Your love so I may shine the light of Your love to others. As You are the author of love I ask for You to teach me how — open my eyes to see and my ears to hear Your gentle leading. In Jesus name, Amen

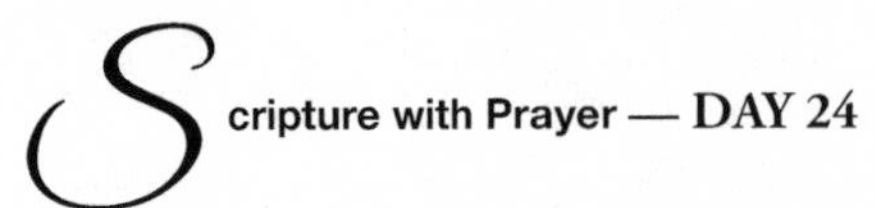

Scripture with Prayer — DAY 24

Beloved, let us love one another, for love is of God;
and everyone who loves is born of God and knows God.
He who does not love does not know God, for God is love.
1 John 4:7-8; - NKJ

Prayer: Heavenly Father, I stand humbly before You asking to know You more intimately — that I may also know Your love more fully, to love others completely. Help me sacrifice my time for the sake of spending it alone with You in Scripture. Guide me with Your Holy Spirit as I meditate on Your Word. Amen

Observation / Reflection

___

___

___

___

Application-Reaction / My Next Steps

___

___

___

___

Prayer / Praise / Promises / Gratitude & Thanksgiving

___

___

___

___

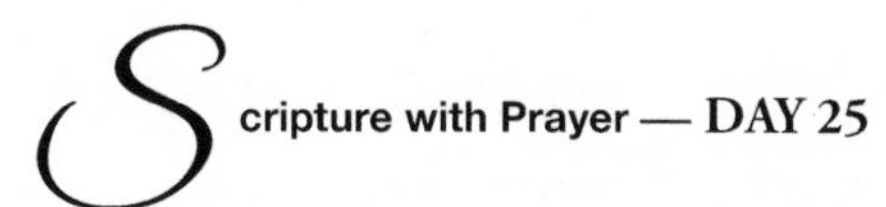

Scripture with Prayer — DAY 25

A new command I give you: Love one another.
As I have loved you, so you must love one another.
By this all men will know that you are my disciples,
if you love one another.
JOHN 13:34-35 - NIV

PRAYER: Jesus, please show me any area of my heart that I need to submit more fully to You, so that Your loving light may shine more brightly through me — to I truly love all fellow believers, and display Your love to the world.

Observation / Reflection

____

____

____

____

Application-Reaction / My Next Steps

____

____

____

____

Prayer / Praise / Promises / Gratitude & Thanksgiving

____

____

____

____

Scripture with Prayer — DAY 26

— Walk in a manner worthy of the calling to which you have been called, with all humility and gentleness, with patience, bearing with one another in love, eager to maintain the unity of the Spirit in the bond of peace. Ephesians 4:1-3 - ESV

Prayer: Holy Lord, in the busyness of my life I find myself drifting from the 'walk' You have designed for me. Give me wisdom to slow down, so I may show to others, all forms of kindness with a peaceful spirit, in the strength You provide — not my own. Eliminate pride in my heart so my service is done in humility.

Observation / Reflection

____

____

____

____

Application-Reaction / My Next Steps

____

____

____

____

Prayer / Praise / Promises / Gratitude & Thanksgiving

____

____

____

____

Scripture with Prayer — DAY 27

For you were called to freedom, brethren; only do not turn your freedom into an opportunity for the flesh, but through love serve one another. For the whole Law is fulfilled in one word, in the statement, "You shall love your neighbor as yourself." But if you bite and devour one another, take care lest you be consumed by one another. But I say, walk by the Spirit, and you will not carry out the desire of the flesh. GALATIANS 5:13-16 - NAS

PRAYER: I ask for a spirit of love and truth. Remove my fleshly tendencies to control or complain. I wish to serve You wholeheartedly and freely, with purity & love. Help me serve others freely, as You also served when You walked the earth.

Observation / Reflection

____

____

____

____

Application-Reaction / My Next Steps

____

____

____

____

Prayer / Praise / Promises / Gratitude & Thanksgiving

____

____

____

____

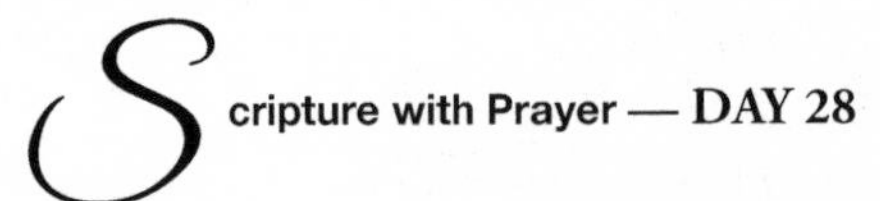

Scripture with Prayer — DAY 28

Let no debt remain outstanding,
except the continuing debt to love one another,
for he who loves his fellowman
has fulfilled the law. Romans 13:8 - NIV

Prayer: Help me to see that since Your Word is eternally true, I don't have to worry or go into debt trying to find things that *I think* will fulfill my heart. In Your presence I truly find extreme fulfillment for everything my heart is looking for, this is motivation to love all others freely, without encumbrance or agitating passions that would distract.

Observation / Reflection

Application-Reaction / My Next Steps

Prayer / Praise / Promises / Gratitude & Thanksgiving

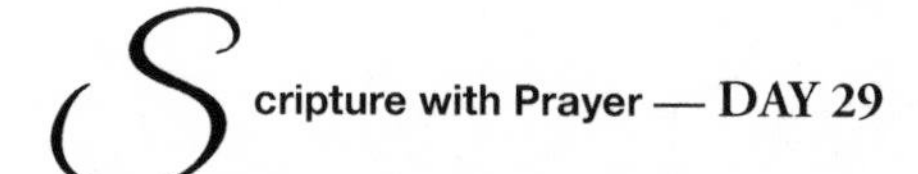

Scripture with Prayer — DAY 29

Beloved, if God so loved us, we also ought to love one another. No one has seen God at any time. If we love one another, God abides in us, and His love has been perfected in us. By this we know that we abide in Him, and He in us, because He has given us of His Spirit.

1 John 4:11-13 - NKJ

Prayer: Lord, help me be a conduit of Your love. Please transform my heart so that my passion is to abide in You, and fulfill Your call to love. Help me eliminate everything that distracts and inhibits me from fulfilling this divine calling.

Observation / Reflection

Application-Reaction / My Next Steps

Prayer / Praise / Promises / Gratitude & Thanksgiving

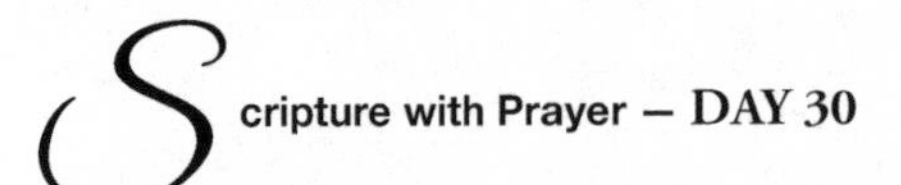

Scripture with Prayer — DAY 30

Having purified your souls by your obedience to the truth for a sincere brotherly love, love one another earnestly from a pure heart, since you have been born again, not of perishable seed but of imperishable, through the living and abiding word of God. 1 PETER 1:22-23 - ESV

PRAYER: Holy Lord, Your eternal Word washes us clean from everything that stands in our way of seeing, hearing, and following You in the path of Your love. Encourage me to be even more diligent to read, study, & obey Your truth, & to love in purity — leading others to Your eternal life and truth.

Observation / Reflection

____

____

____

____

Application-Reaction / My Next Steps

____

____

____

____

Prayer / Praise / Promises / Gratitude & Thanksgiving

____

____

____

____

Scripture with Prayer — DAY 31

May the Lord make your love increase and overflow for each other and for everyone else, just as ours does for you. May he strengthen your hearts so that you will be blameless and holy in the presence of our God and Father when our Lord Jesus comes with all his holy ones. — Now about your love for one another we do not need to write to you, for you yourselves have been taught by God to love each other. 1 THESSALONIANS 3:12-13; 4:9 — NIV

PRAYER: Your Spirit will guide me in loving others. Help focus my eyes firmly on You throughout the day, so that I will consciously be aware of Your leading. So as I become firmly rooted in You, my love will increase & overflow!

Observation / Reflection

Application-Reaction / My Next Steps

Prayer / Praise / Promises / Gratitude & Thanksgiving

Scripture with Prayer — DAY 32

Let us hold unswervingly to the hope we profess, for he who promised is faithful. And let us consider how we may spur one another on toward love and good deeds, not giving up meeting together, as some are in the habit of doing, but encouraging one another—and all the more as you see the Day approaching. **HEBREW 1: 23-25 —NIV**

PRAYER: Help me, oh Lord, to see that I need other believers and they also need me. With a solid faith in Your hope, I ask for a renewed sense of commitment to help others in their faith! Help me feel the joy of relationships within Your family.

Observation / Reflection

____

____

____

____

Application-Reaction / My Next Steps

____

____

____

____

Prayer / Praise / Promises / Gratitude & Thanksgiving

____

____

____

____

Scripture with Prayer — DAY 33

My goal is that they may be encouraged in heart and united in love, so that they may have the full riches of complete understanding, in order that they may know the mystery of God, namely, Christ, in whom are hidden all the treasures of wisdom and knowledge.

— So then, just as you received Christ Jesus as Lord, continue to live your lives in him. COLOSSIANS 2:2-3,6 NIV

PRAYER: Jesus, my obedience to You, to love You and others, is required for me to have full understanding of Your wisdom and knowledge. Strengthen & nurture my love, so that I stand united with Your people, to live my life in You.

Observation / Reflection

____

____

____

____

Application-Reaction / My Next Steps

____

____

____

____

Prayer / Praise / Promises / Gratitude & Thanksgiving

____

____

____

____

OUR LOVE FOR GOD (DAY 34 - 47)

Loving God is our greatest joy, He abides with those who love Him.
John 15

PRAYER OF ST. RICHARD OF CHICHESTER
Most merciful Redeemer, Friend and Brother,
may we know you more clearly, love you more dearly,
and follow you more nearly, day by day.
Amen.

POEM OF LOVE FOR GOD —Johann Schaffer, 1657
Thee will I love, my Strength and Tower;
Thee will I love, my Hope, my Joy;
Thee will I love and praise forever,
For never shall Thy kindness end;
Thee will I love, O Light Divine,
So long as life is mine.

PRAYER
Heavenly Father, I am so very thankful that You have blessed me with the ability to feel Your loving compassion toward me personally! And so I am filled with joy and peace. And it gives me confidence to walk through this week knowing I am not alone. Help me to become ever more aware of Your loving presence through every minute of each day, so that my joy may be complete in You! In Jesus Name, Amen.

Scripture with Prayer — DAY 34

"Teacher, which is the greatest commandment in the Law?" Jesus replied: "'Love the Lord your God with all your heart and with all your soul and with all your mind. This is the first and greatest commandment." MATTHEW 22:36-37 - NIV

PRAYER: Please show me how to love You with all my heart, as my highest priority. Things that seem urgent tend to take precedence in my life. Help me simplify my life to make space and time to spend with You — to be in Your presence, to know and love You in truth.

Observation / Reflection

Application-Reaction / My Next Steps

Prayer / Praise / Promises / Gratitude & Thanksgiving

Scripture with Prayer — DAY 35

Only be very careful to observe the commandment and the law which Moses the servant of the LORD commanded you, to love the LORD your God and walk in all His ways and keep His commandments and hold fast to Him and serve Him with all your heart and with all your soul. *Joshua 22:5 - NAS*

Prayer: Father, if proof of my love is obeying Your commandments, to love You and others, then this day I intentionally renew my desire to walk ever-nearer to You. I admit that to truly love, I need Your Divine guidance. My eyes are on You, please guide my steps. I commit myself into Your loving arms.

Observation / Reflection

Application-Reaction / My Next Steps

Prayer / Praise / Promises / Gratitude & Thanksgiving

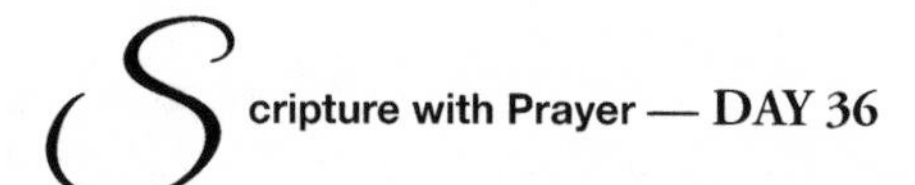

Scripture with Prayer — DAY 36

O love the LORD, all you His godly ones!
The LORD preserves the faithful,
And fully recompenses the proud doer.
Be strong, and let your heart take courage,
All you who hope in the LORD.
Psalm 31: 23-24

Prayer: I love You Lord, You preserve me in my trials. When others seem to be against me, You give my heart strength & hope. Please conform me into Your image, and give me strength to obey. I worship You, Almighty King!

Observation / Reflection

Application-Reaction / My Next Steps

Prayer / Praise / Promises / Gratitude & Thanksgiving

Scripture with Prayer — DAY 37

I Love you, O LORD, my strength. The LORD is my rock and my fortress and my deliverer, My God, my rock, in whom I take refuge; My shield and the horn of my salvation, my stronghold. Psalm 18:1-2 - ESV

Prayer: Lord, the vision of You as my fortress, rock, shield, and deliverer, my glorious Savior means You are higher than my trouble, failures, losses, fret, and worry. Help me this day enter into the place of holy calm, peace, and stillness, where the fullness of Your presence dwells.

Observation / Reflection

____

____

____

____

Application-Reaction / My Next Steps

____

____

____

____

Prayer / Praise / Promises / Gratitude & Thanksgiving

____

____

____

____

Scripture with Prayer — DAY 38

If anyone says, "I love God," and hates his brother, he is a liar; for the one who does not love his brother whom he has seen, cannot love God whom he has not seen. And this commandment we have from Him; whoever loves God must also love his brother. 1 John 4:20-21 - ESV

PRAYER: Heavenly Father, help me to see that I cannot claim to love you yet have ill feelings toward others. Particularly those members of Your family (the church). I ask for Your Holy Spirit to show me specific areas in my heart that need to be 'cut-away', so that You may shine Your love through me unhindered by darkness.

Observation / Reflection

____

____

____

____

Application-Reaction / My Next Steps

____

____

____

____

Prayer / Praise / Promises / Gratitude & Thanksgiving

____

____

____

____

Scripture with Prayer — DAY 39

— So when they had finished breakfast, Jesus said to Simon Peter, "Simon, son of John, do you love Me more than these?" He said to Him, "Yes, Lord; You know that I love You." He said to him,

"Tend My lambs." . . . "Shepherd My sheep." . . . "Tend My sheep."

JOHN 21: 15-17

PRAYER: The degree of my love for You, oh Lord, is evident by the extent I willingly tend & feed Your tender lambs and sheep. Lambs have special needs requiring extra attention. If lambs are not fed and tended to with care, they become week adult sheep with poor appetites. Oh, Give me an increasing love for your lambs & sheep, that I may lovingly serve You by serving them.

Observation / Reflection

____

____

____

____

Application-Reaction / My Next Steps

____

____

____

____

Prayer / Praise / Promises / Gratitude & Thanksgiving

____

____

____

____

Scripture with Prayer — DAY 40

SHOWING WE LOVE GOD THROUGH OBEDIENCE

and walk in love, just as Christ also loved you and gave Himself up for us, an offering and a sacrifice to God as a fragrant aroma. — If you love Me you will keep my commandments.

EPHESIANS 5:2: JOHN 14:15

PRAYER: Lord, I love You dearly. I long to be fully obedient to You by walking in love. At times this is hard for me, and as a sacrifice I lay down my rights to justify myself, or deny others love because of fear. Grant me strength to submit to love.

Observation / Reflection

___

___

___

___

Application-Reaction / My Next Steps

___

___

___

___

Prayer / Praise / Promises / Gratitude & Thanksgiving

___

___

___

___

Scripture with Prayer — DAY 41

JESUS TEACHES: LOVE OF MONEY WILL PREVENT OUR LOVE FOR GOD:

No one can serve two masters. For you will hate one and love the other; you will be devoted to one and despise the other. You cannot serve God and be enslaved to money.

MATTHEW 6:24 — NLT

PRAYER: Father, I confess there were times I placed a higher priority on acquiring money than seeking communion with You. Please forgive me. Again, I submit myself to Your care and love. Help me to love You aright in spirit and in truth.

Observation / Reflection

Application-Reaction / My Next Steps

Prayer / Praise / Promises / Gratitude & Thanksgiving

Scripture with Prayer — DAY 42

If we Truly Love Christ, We Will Take Up Our Cross

Then Jesus said to His disciples, "If anyone wishes to come after Me, he must deny himself, and take up his cross and follow Me. For whoever wishes to save his life will lose it; but whoever loses his life for My sake will find it. For what will it profit a man if he gains the whole world and forfeits his soul? Or what will a man give in exchange for his soul? Matthew 16:24-26

Prayer: Jesus, I wish to show You my love by sacrificing my own pleasures for the sake of Your work. loving You is my top priority. It is a great honor! I wish to serve You by following and taking up my Cross — please show me my next steps.

Observation / Reflection

Application-Reaction / My Next Steps

Prayer / Praise / Promises / Gratitude & Thanksgiving

Scripture with Prayer — DAY 43 - His Names Are Precious to Us

Let my beloved come into his garden and taste its choice fruits... Your name is like perfume poured out. - Therefore, to you who believe, He is precious.
Song of Songs 1:3,4:16; 1 Peter 2:7 - NKJ

And His name will be called Wonderful, — and His name is called The Word of God. And on His robe and on His thigh He has a name written, "KING OF KINGS, AND LORD OF LORDS." Isaiah 9:6; Revelation 19:13,16 - NKJ

Prayer: Oh Lord Jesus, I love You! You are wonderful to me, all your names are precious in my site. They are like perfume to my spirit, they are salvation to my soul.

Observation / Reflection

____

____

____

____

Application-Reaction / My Next Steps

____

____

____

____

Prayer / Praise / Promises / Gratitude & Thanksgiving

____

____

____

____

Scripture with Prayer — DAY 44

My meditation of him shall be sweet: I will be glad in the Lord... O how I love Your law! It is my meditation all the day. Psalm 104:34; 119:97

Jesus answered and said to him, "If anyone loves Me, he will keep My word; and My Father will love him, and We will come to him and make Our abode with him. John 14:23

Prayer: Jesus, Your Word and commandments are sweet to my ear. My mind and heart are directed toward keeping Your law of love. Come into my heart, I love to have Your peace-giving presence with me all the day long!

Observation / Reflection

Application-Reaction / My Next Steps

Prayer / Praise / Promises / Gratitude & Thanksgiving

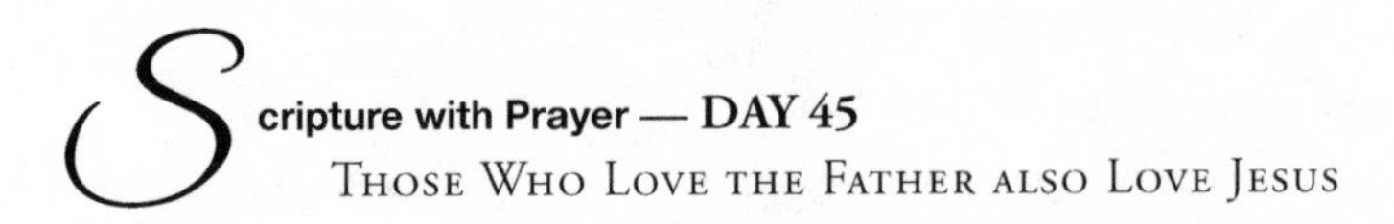

Scripture with Prayer — DAY 45

Those Who Love the Father also Love Jesus

Jesus told them, "If God were your Father, you would love me, because I have come to you from God. I am not here on my own, but he sent me." — "for the Father himself loves you dearly because you love me and believe that I came from God." John 8:42;16:27

Prayer: Help me accept the mystery of Your Trinity, Oh Lord. I say I love You, but if there are miss-understandings or incorrect ideas of You within my heart, please reveal them. Help me make corrections so my love for You continues to grow. Wash me in the truth of Your Word and strengthen my Love for You.

Observation / Reflection

___

___

___

___

Application-Reaction / My Next Steps

___

___

___

___

Prayer / Praise / Promises / Gratitude & Thanksgiving

___

___

___

___

Scripture with Prayer — DAY 46

When Jesus walked the earth, He loved our Father dearly and loved to spend time with Him — He is our example:

Very early in the morning, while it was still dark,
Jesus got up, left the house and went off to a solitary place, where he prayed.
Mark 1:35 - NIV

Prayer: In Your presence is the fullness of Joy, oh Lord. As Jesus taught how to seek Your intimate company, I too wish to earnestly do the same. I love You, help it be my passion to seek a life lived every moment in communion with You.

Observation / Reflection

Application-Reaction / My Next Steps

Prayer / Praise / Promises / Gratitude & Thanksgiving

Scripture with Prayer — DAY 47

And we know that in all things God works for the good of those who love him, who have been called according to his purpose. —in all these things we are more than conquerors through him who loved us. Romans 8:28,37 — NIV

Prayer: Lord, I rest on Your Word today and am at peace knowing that all situations in my life are working toward my good… and so that I will fulfill the ultimate Divine purpose You have designed for my life. I ask that You increase my faith so that my love for You is also strengthened in all things.

Observation / Reflection

Application-Reaction / My Next Steps

Prayer / Praise / Promises / Gratitude & Thanksgiving

JOY (DAYS 48 - 69)

Rejoice in the Lord always: and again I say, Rejoice. Philippians 4:4

ANCIENT POEM OF GOD'S JOY — **Michael Schirmer, 1640**

O Holy Spirit, enter in and in our hearts Your work begin,
Your temple sure to make us; Sun of the soul, Your Light Divine,
Around and in us brightly shine, to joy and gladness wake us,
That we, in You truly living, to You giving prayer unceasing,
May in love be still increasing

O gentle Dew, from heaven, now fall with power upon the hearts of all,
Your tender love instilling, that heart to heart more closely bound,
In kindly deeds be fruitful found, the law of love fulfilling,
Dwell thus in us; Envy banish; strife will vanish where You live.
Peace and love and joy You gives us.

PRAYER

My Father, as Your child, I am encouraged when thinking how You delight in me. Your Fatherly joy fills my heart with warmth. As my loving Father, You smile lovingly and rejoice even over my small steps. When I stumble learning from my mistakes, Your compassion brings comfort and assurance.

Your Delight in me brings joy and gladness! Let me ever be filled with joy, that You drew me with bands of kindness, that Your love for me is assured. Help me to draw nearer to Your joyful presence. Amen

Scripture with Prayer — DAY 48

THE CLOSER WE ABIDE IN HIM THE DEEPER OUR JOY:

— ***Do not be grieved, for the joy of the Lord is your strength.*** NEHEMIAH 8:10

"I am the true vine...Abide in Me and I in you...These things I have spoken to you, that My joy may remain in you, and that that your joy may be full." JOHN 15:1,4,11 - KJV

PRAYER: Heavenly Father, Your presence truly fills me with unexplainable joy! I have seen how abiding in You fills me with great delight! Show me the great depths of Your life within me, so that I may always draw from this well.

Observation / Reflection

____

____

____

____

Application-Reaction / My Next Steps

____

____

____

____

Prayer / Praise / Promises / Gratitude & Thanksgiving

____

____

____

____

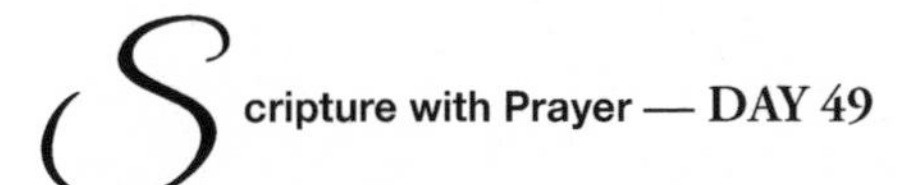

Scripture with Prayer — DAY 49

But the fruit of the Spirit is love, joy, peace, forbearance, kindness, goodness, faithfulness, gentleness and self-control. Against such things there is no law. Those who belong to Christ Jesus have crucified the flesh with its passions and desires. Since we live by the Spirit, let us keep in step with the Spirit.

GALATIANS 5:22-25 - NAS

PRAYER: Jesus, I am walking in freedom & fellowship with Your Holy Spirit. In kindness and goodness You have drawn me out of a dark land of bondage, ruled by fleshly passions that deny Your existence. I give these up willingly to live in Your joy.

Observation / Reflection

Application-Reaction / My Next Steps

Prayer / Praise / Promises / Gratitude & Thanksgiving

Scripture with Prayer — DAY 50

In all this you greatly rejoice, though now for a little while you may have had to suffer grief in all kinds of trials. — But rejoice inasmuch as you participate in the sufferings of Christ, so that you may be overjoyed when his glory is revealed. *1 Peter 1:6; 4:13 — NIV*

Prayer: I have chosen to follow You Jesus, and You promised trials for those who walk in the way of Your cross. Today I look also to Your promise of joy for those who abide in You… I ask for greater faith in You, so I too can rejoice in trials and sufferings. Help me keep my eyes on You!

Observation / Reflection

___

___

___

___

Application-Reaction / My Next Steps

___

___

___

___

Prayer / Praise / Promises / Gratitude & Thanksgiving

___

___

___

___

Scripture with Prayer — DAY 51

When anxiety was great within me, your consolation brought me joy. —You have put gladness in my heart, more than when their grain and new wine abound. PSALM 94:19; 4: 7 — NAS

I pray for them… I will remain in the world no longer, but they are still in the world,… Holy Father, protect them by the power of your name… so that they may be one as we are one… I am coming to you now, but I say these things while I am still in the world, so that they may have the full measure of my joy within them. JOHN 17:9,11,13 - NIV

PRAYER: Jesus, thank You! I extend my deepest gratitude that You made me to have ability to feel Your joy, and You have made a way for that to happen! I lay down my anxieties & cares in faith, I no longer put faith in worry, but in You!

Observation / Reflection

____

____

____

____

Application-Reaction / My Next Steps

____

____

____

____

Prayer / Praise / Promises / Gratitude & Thanksgiving

____

____

____

____

Scripture with Prayer — DAY 52

Shout joyfully to the Lord, all the earth.
Serve the Lord with gladness; Come before Him with joyful singing.
Know that the Lord Himself is God;
It is He who has made us, and not we ourselves;
We are His people and the sheep of His pasture.
Enter His gates with thanksgiving, and His courts with praise.
Give thanks to Him, bless His name. For the Lord is good;
His lovingkindness is everlasting,
and His faithfulness to all generations. PSALM 100 - NAS

PRAYER: Oh Lord, I cannot count the blessings of Your presence — extreme peace and joy fill me. My heart is filled with thanksgiving and praise to You.

Observation / Reflection

___

___

___

___

Application-Reaction / My Next Steps

___

___

___

___

Prayer / Praise / Promises / Gratitude & Thanksgiving

___

___

___

___

Scripture with Prayer — DAY 53

Joy of the Redeemed

The desert and the parched land will be glad; the wilderness will rejoice and blossom. Like the crocus, it will burst into bloom; it will rejoice greatly and shout for joy. The glory of Lebanon will be given to it, the splendor of Carmel and Sharon; they will see the glory of the Lord, the splendor of our God. — everlasting joy will crown their heads. Gladness and joy will overtake them, and sorrow and sighing will flee away. Isaiah 35:1-2,10

Prayer: Hope of Your glory frees me to live happily today! Help me see & release to you those things I am trying to control or worry about. I joy in You.

Observation / Reflection

___

___

___

___

Application-Reaction / My Next Steps

___

___

___

___

Prayer / Praise / Promises / Gratitude & Thanksgiving

___

___

___

___

Scripture with Prayer — DAY 54

I will rejoice greatly in the Lord, My soul will exult in my God; For He has clothed me with garments of salvation, He has wrapped me with a robe of righteousness, As a bridegroom decks himself with a garland, And as a bride adorns herself with her jewels. ... And as the bridegroom rejoices over the bride, So your God will rejoice over you. ISAIAH 61:10: 62:5

PRAYER: It brings me joy, knowing our relationship is as close, comforting, and secure as that of a bride & bridegroom. Pondering that true intimate love, I walk in the delight thinking of the day when this promise will be fulfilled! My heart is filled with gratitude. Thank You Lord, for the promises in Your Word.

Observation / Reflection

Application-Reaction / My Next Steps

Prayer / Praise / Promises / Gratitude & Thanksgiving

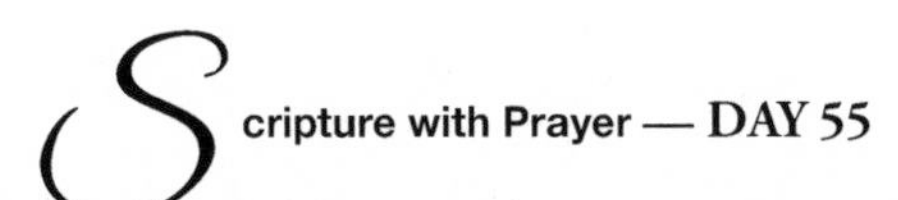

Scripture with Prayer — DAY 55

May the God of hope fill you
with all joy and peace as you trust in him,
so that you may overflow with hope by the power
of the Holy Spirit. Romans 15:13 - NIV

Prayer: Heavenly Father, I ask that Your joy & peace overflow from my spirit so that others see it — in the power and strength of Your Holy Spirit within me. My heart-desire is to bless them by the out-flow of Your presence!

Observation / Reflection

___

___

___

___

Application-Reaction / My Next Steps

___

___

___

___

Prayer / Praise / Promises / Gratitude & Thanksgiving

___

___

___

___

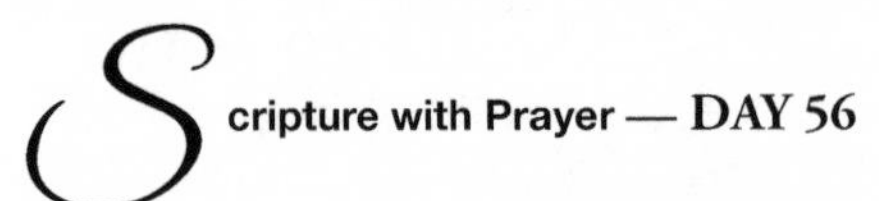

Scripture with Prayer — DAY 56

[Jesus] .. through whom we have gained access by faith
into this grace in which we now stand.
And we rejoice in the hope of the glory of God.
ROMANS 5:2 - NIV

PRAYER: Lord, sometimes I feel weak. Help me stand firmly today upon Your grace in faith. Then I will find hope to rejoice in Your glorious promises. Forgive me for trying to solve my problems without You. I truly desire to live by faith in You for everything in my life. My accomplishments are nothing without You!

Observation / Reflection

Application-Reaction / My Next Steps

Prayer / Praise / Promises / Gratitude & Thanksgiving

Scripture with Prayer — DAY 57

Rejoice with those who rejoice; mourn with those who mourn.
Romans 12:15

Always be full of joy in the Lord. I say it again—rejoice! Let everyone see that you are considerate in all you do. Remember, the Lord is coming soon. Philippians 4:4-5 — NIV

Prayer: Please help me to always maintain a positive considerate attitude that rejoices with others. Being filled with Your joy is my goal! I would like to be a witness for You in everything I do — I will obey and submit to Your guidance.

Observation / Reflection

Application-Reaction / My Next Steps

Prayer / Praise / Promises / Gratitude & Thanksgiving

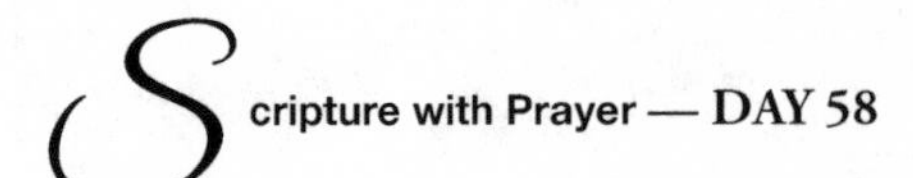

Scripture with Prayer — DAY 58

Praise be to the God and Father of our Lord Jesus Christ! In his great mercy he has given us new birth into a living hope through the resurrection of Jesus Christ from the dead, and into an inheritance that can never perish, spoil or fade-- kept in heaven for you.
1 Peter 1:3-4 - NIV

Prayer: I will praise Your with great joy and thanksgiving, that You have made a way for me to spend eternal life with You through Jesus shed blood. He is my living hope, resurrected from the dead, and eternal life! I praise You Holy Name!

Observation / Reflection

____

____

____

____

Application-Reaction / My Next Steps

____

____

____

____

Prayer / Praise / Promises / Gratitude & Thanksgivinge

____

____

____

____

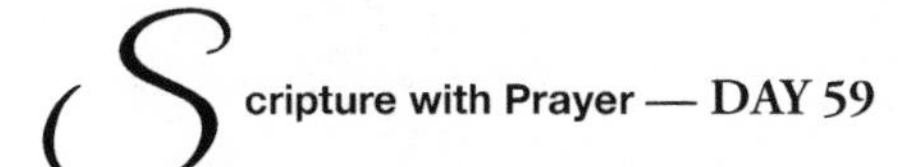

Scripture with Prayer — DAY 59

. . . Rejoicing in hope. — faith and love that spring from the hope stored up for you in heaven, and about which you have already heard in the true message of the gospel.

ROMANS 12:1 - KJV; COLOSSIANS 1:5 - NIV

PRAYER: By faith, I rejoice because Your Word declares the goodness of eternal life upon us! I am free to sing in jubilance, dancing in my heart before our loving King! — Help this be true in my mind and spirit today, oh heavenly Father.

O *bservation / Reflection*

A *pplication-Reaction / My Next Steps*

P *rayer / Praise / Promises / Gratitude & Thanksgiving*

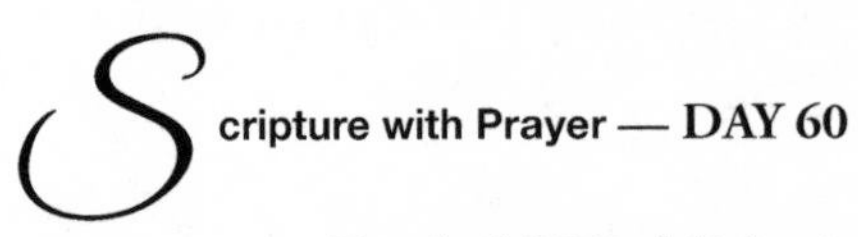

Scripture with Prayer — DAY 60

For the LORD delights in you, Isaiah 62:4 - NKJ

The Lord your God is with you, the Mighty Warrior who saves.
He will take great delight in you; in his love he will . . .
will rejoice over you with singing. Zephaniah 3:17 — NIV

Prayer: Holy God, I am ever amazed that you long to share Your joy with us in a personal way! I humbly ask that You enrich me with that same delight! You created me to be Your friend, give me a fresh awareness of Your Spirit within me!

Observation / Reflection

___

___

___

___

Application-Reaction / My Next Steps

___

___

___

___

Prayer / Praise / Promises / Gratitude & Thanksgiving

___

___

___

___

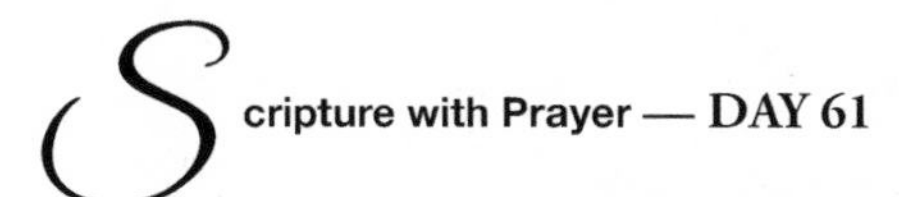

Scripture with Prayer — DAY 61

The LORD delights in those who..,
who put their hope in his unfailing love.
Psalm 147:11 - NIV

Prayer: Heavenly Father, Let it be true this day that I put my hope fully in Your unfailing love! I desire that no other insufficient worldly pleasure take Your place in my heart. Direct my steps to eliminate what I have relied on in the past, to set my passions on what truly satisfies — Your in me, my hope & true joy!

Observation / Reflection

Application-Reaction / My Next Steps

Prayer / Praise / Promises / Gratitude & Thanksgiving

Scripture with Prayer — DAY 62

"My delights were with the sons of men."

— looking unto Jesus, the author and finisher of our faith,

who for the joy that was set before Him endured the cross, despising the shame, and has sat down at the right hand of the throne of God.

PROVERBS 8:31; HEBREWS 12:2 - KJV

PRAYER: Jesus, thank You for having delight in being with us & coming down from Your glorious heavenly home to experience the worst form of abuse possible — because You longed to have us with You in Heaven. I feel deep joy & gratitude for Your sacrifice. You suffered for the joy, help me do the same in service to You.

Observation / Reflection

____

____

____

____

Application-Reaction / My Next Steps

____

____

____

____

Prayer / Praise / Promises / Gratitude & Thanksgiving

____

____

____

____

Scripture with Prayer — DAY 63

O God, you are my God; earnestly I seek you; My soul thirsts for you; my flesh faints for you, as in a dry and weary land where there is no water. When I remember you upon my bed, and meditate on you in the watches of the night; For you have been my help, and in the shadow of your wings I will sing for joy. My soul clings to you; your right hand upholds me.
PSALM 63:1;6-8 - ESV

PRAYER: Father, it is right and needful that I set my passions and desires upon You alone. It is Your divine purpose and path that will be true joy! Instead of spending time just to be with You, I have pursued my own pleasures and goals, and they have left me empty. Renew my passion to be with You, and enjoy You.

Observation / Reflection

Application-Reaction / My Next Steps

Prayer / Praise / Promises / Gratitude & Thanksgiving

Scripture with Prayer — DAY 64

Make a joyful noise to the Lord, all the earth;
break forth into joyous song and sing praises!

Sing praises to the Lord with the lyre, with the lyre and the sound of melody! With trumpets and the sound of the horn make a joyful noise before the King, the Lord! PSALM 98: 4-6 - ESV

PRAYER: The revelation of You as King and Lord of my life has brought delight and singing to my heart. When I stray, my joy decreases. Today I will take a fresh audit of my heart & intentions to see if You reign supremely. whether I allow your rule over my words & thoughts? Help me be honest & provide Your wisdom, guidance, and love as I traverse the hidden areas of my soul.

Observation / Reflection

___

___

___

___

Application-Reaction / My Next Steps

___

___

___

___

Prayer / Praise / Promises / Gratitude & Thanksgiving

___

___

___

___

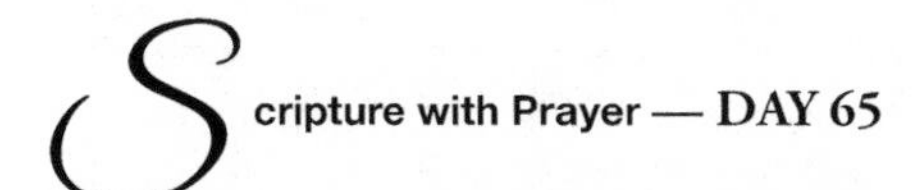

Scripture with Prayer — DAY 65

Rejoice in the LORD, O you righteous!
For praise from the upright is beautiful.
Psalm 33:1 - NKJ

Prayer: Today I ask that You help me put on the beautiful garment of rejoicing and praise! Help me focus today to seek understand of *how* to truly praise You — to praise You in spirit and in truth. As Jesus taught, "…true worshipers will worship the Father in spirit and in truth. The Father is looking for those who will worship him that way." (John 4:23)

Observation / Reflection

____
____
____
____

Application-Reaction / My Next Steps

____
____
____
____

Prayer / Praise / Promises / Gratitude & Thanksgiving

____
____
____
____

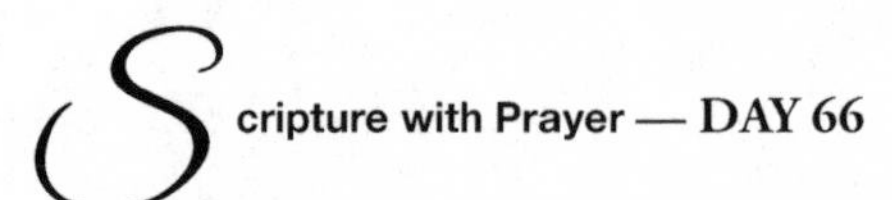

Scripture with Prayer — DAY 66

As he was drawing near—already on the way down the Mount of Olives—the whole multitude of his disciples began to rejoice and praise God with a loud voice for all the mighty works that they had seen, saying, "Blessed is the King who comes in the name of the Lord! Peace in heaven and glory in the highest!"

LUKE 19:37-38 - ESV

PRAYER: Jesus my blessed King, Your Word says that You inhabit the praises of Your people. And in Your Presence is the fullness of joy. I humbly ask once again, help me praise You in spirit and in truth, just as those who sang out during Your Triumphant Entry into Jerusalem!

Observation / Reflection

Application-Reaction / My Next Steps

Prayer / Praise / Promises / Gratitude & Thanksgiving

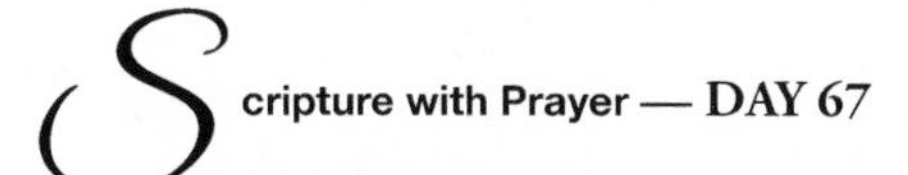

Scripture with Prayer — DAY 67

Blessed are the people who know the joyful sound! They walk, O LORD, in the light of Your countenance. In Your name they rejoice all day long, And in Your righteousness they are exalted. For You are the glory of their strength, And in Your favor our horn is exalted.

PSALM 89:15-17 - NKJ

Prayer: Heavenly Father, if I walk every day 'in the light of Your countenance', all my worries and concerns will fade away in Your glory! Help me to walk today in this way, with my eyes focused on You it will be impossible for me to stumble!

Observation / Reflection

___

___

___

___

Application-Reaction / My Next Steps

___

___

___

___

Prayer / Praise / Promises / Gratitude & Thanksgiving

___

___

___

___

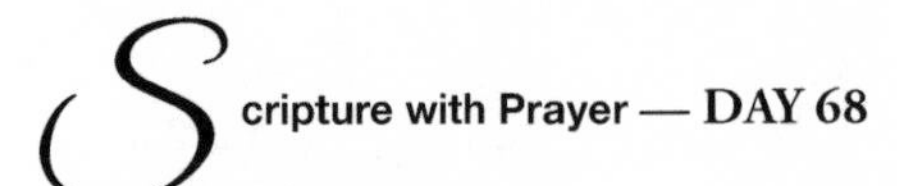

Scripture with Prayer — DAY 68

I have seen you in the sanctuary and beheld your power and your glory.
Because your love is better than life, my lips will glorify you.
I will praise you as long as I live, and in your name I will lift up my hands.
My soul will be satisfied as with the richest of foods;
with singing lips my mouth will praise you. PSALM 63:2-5 - NIV

Prayer: Father, Thank you for King David's timeless example of how to walk in faith, hope, and joy! In faith today, I claim 'Your love is better than life'. Because You feed me in the richness of Your Word, my heart is filled with joyful praise.

O*bservation / Reflection*

A*pplication-Reaction / My Next Steps*

P*rayer / Praise / Promises / Gratitude & Thanksgiving*

Scripture with Prayer — DAY 69

JESUS SAID OF ABRAHAM:

Your father Abraham rejoiced as he looked forward to my coming. He saw it and was glad." JOHN 8:56

LET US ALSO REJOICE & BE GLAD AS WE LOOK FORWARD TO HIS SECOND COMING!

Let us be glad and rejoice, and let us give honor to him. For the time has come for the wedding feast of the Lamb, and his bride has prepared herself. REVELATION 19:9

Prayer: Jesus, I am excited about seeing You at the wedding feast You are preparing for us! Help me to walk out these last days with the joyful purpose of spreading the good news of Your amazing offer of grace and eternal life to others!

Observation / Reflection

___

___

___

___

Application-Reaction / My Next Steps

___

___

___

___

Prayer / Praise / Promises / Gratitude & Thanksgiving

___

___

___

___

PEACE (DAYS 70 - 90)

Peace is a way of life, His name is Jesus – Those who walk in Him have unexplainable peace

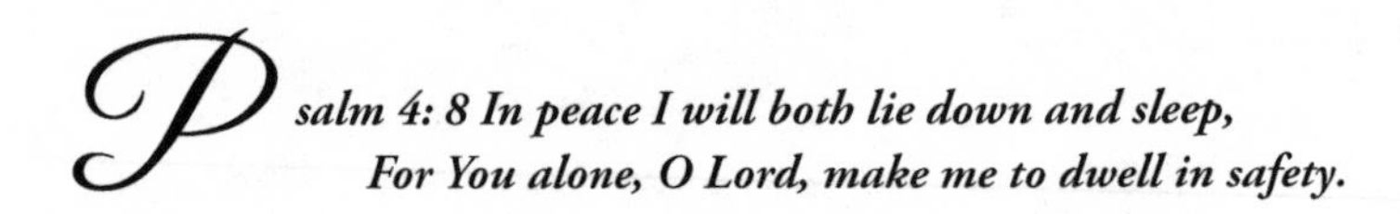

Psalm 4: 8 In peace I will both lie down and sleep,
For You alone, O Lord, make me to dwell in safety.

When peace like a river attendeth my way,
when sorrows like sea billows roll;
whatever my lot, thou hast taught me to say,
"It is well, it is well with my soul."

Though Satan should buffet, though trials should come,
let this blest assurance control:
that Christ has regarded my helpless estate,
and has shed his own blood for my soul.
Horatio Gates Spafford, 1873

PRAYER Attributed to Francis of Assisi

Lord, make me an instrument of your peace. Where there is hatred, let me sow love; Where there is injury, pardon; Where there is doubt, faith; Where there is despair, hope; Where there is darkness, light; Where there is sadness, joy.
O Divine Master, grant that we may not so much seek to be consoled as to console; Not so much to be understood as to understand; Not so much to be loved as to love. For it is in giving that we receive, it is in pardoning that we are pardoned, it is in dying that we are born to eternal life.

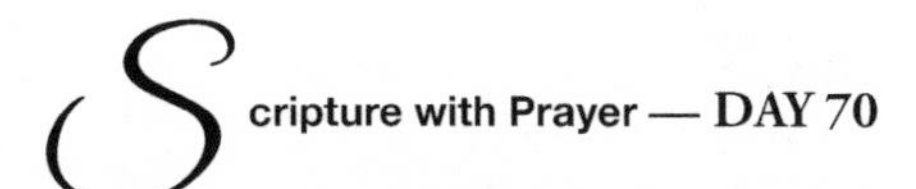

Scripture with Prayer — DAY 70

Peace I leave with you; My peace I give to you; not as the world gives, do I give to you. Let not your heart be troubled, nor let it be fearful. JOHN 14:27 - NAS

PRAYER: Jesus, You are like my resting place — I find peace and serenity in You. I now see that the busy chaos of accumulating 'things' and trying to find fulfillment elsewhere has me in turmoil. Guide my steps in submission to Your continuous abiding love, to stop searching for worldly solutions, to live fully in You. I need Your peace oh Lord, encompass my life today. Please let me feel You so that I can sense Your peace within me all the day long. Thank You!

Observation / Reflection

____

____

____

____

Application-Reaction / My Next Steps

____

____

____

____

Prayer / Praise / Promises / Gratitude & Thanksgiving

____

____

____

____

Scripture with Prayer — DAY 71

For God is not a God of confusion but of peace. 1 Corinthians 14:33 — ***For our struggle is not against flesh and blood*** *[contending only with physical opponents]*, ***but against the rulers, against the powers, against the world forces of this*** *[present]* ***darkness, against the spiritual forces of wickedness in the heavenly*** *(supernatural)* ***places.*** Ephesians 6:12 - AMP

Prayer: As I reflect on Your peace today, I realize how much I have been doubting the truth of it. And my mind has been focused on the physical issues and desires in my life. Forgive me for not setting my faith upon Your promise of peace, for relying on my own learned beliefs that rule my mind & heart. Help me walk in vibrant spiritual relationship with You, to overshadow any benefits from physical pleasures & worries, so I may have Your extreme peace I desire!

Observation / Reflection

____

Application-Reaction / My Next Steps

____

Prayer / Praise / Promises / Gratitude & Thanksgiving

____

Scripture with Prayer — DAY 72

Do not be anxious about anything, but in everything, by prayer and petition, with thanksgiving, present your requests to God. And the peace of God, which transcends all understanding, will guard your hearts and your minds in Christ Jesus. PHILIPPIANS 4:6-7 - NIV

PRAYER: Increase my faith, oh Lord, and help me claim your promise of peace. By Your Holy Spirit, help me to intentionally replace feelings and beliefs of anxiety and worry. Instead, fill my mind with Your Word and promises, that in faith, I stand upon them today! You gave me Your peace, but I have not been diligent to intentionally obey & 'walk in it'! I choose to seek with all my heart, that deep relationship with You, to replace thoughts & images in my mind that steal precious moments with You. Help me walk-out this commitment today.

Observation / Reflection

____

____

____

____

Application-Reaction / My Next Steps

____

____

____

____

Prayer / Praise / Promises / Gratitude & Thanksgiving

____

____

____

____

Scripture with Prayer — DAY 73

For thus the Lord God, the Holy One of Israel, has said, "In repentance and rest you shall be saved, In quietness and trust is your strength." - In peace I will lie down and sleep, for you alone, Lord, make me dwell in safety. ISAIAH 30:15; PSALM 4:8 - NAS

PRAYER: Holy Most High God, You require us to have faith in You alone — that we seek our peace and safety from You only. I need Your Divine presence & peace in my life, to help me quiet my anxious spirit. It will give me a resting-trust in You. Please increase my peace in You, then in strong faith I will abide in Your peace all day long, in quiet confidence and assurance my sleep will be sweet.

Observation / Reflection

____

____

____

____

Application-Reaction / My Next Steps

____

____

____

____

Prayer / Praise / Promises / Gratitude & Thanksgiving

____

____

____

____

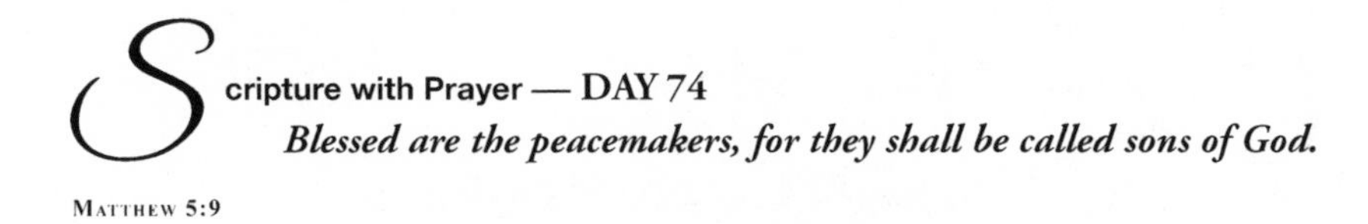

Blessed are the peacemakers, for they shall be called sons of God.

MATTHEW 5:9

Great peace have those who love your law,
and nothing can make them stumble.
PSALM 119:165 - NAS

PRAYER: Lord, Help me to love You and Your Word with greater passion and desire, that I earnestly spend 'time' to seek both with great hunger of heart. I ask that in doing so, You will transform my mind and heart, and cause me to walk more fully in Your pathway of peace. Make me a 'peace-maker'.

Observation / Reflection

____

____

____

____

Application-Reaction / My Next Steps

____

____

____

____

Prayer / Praise / Promises / Gratitude & Thanksgiving

____

____

____

____

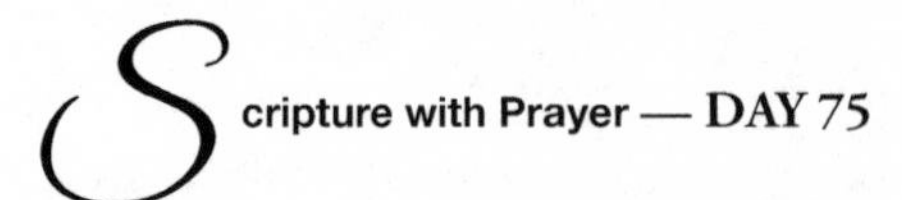

Scripture with Prayer — DAY 75

For the mind set on the flesh is death,
but the mind set on the Spirit is life and peace.
Romans 8:6 - NAS

PRAYER: Holy God, There is no true peace in pleasures apart from You. It is the temporary worldly 'seemingly okay' pleasures that tend to pull me away from Your Spirit, Your true life, and Your true peace. Help me to discern the difference. Your way of true life is the narrow spiritual pathway, help me set my heart on sacrifice, to let go of everything that separates me from Your peaceful loving Spirit. Thank You for opening my eyes, my heart is filled with gratitude.

Observation / Reflection

____
____
____
____

Application-Reaction / My Next Steps

____
____
____
____

Prayer / Praise / Promises / Gratitude & Thanksgiving

____
____
____
____

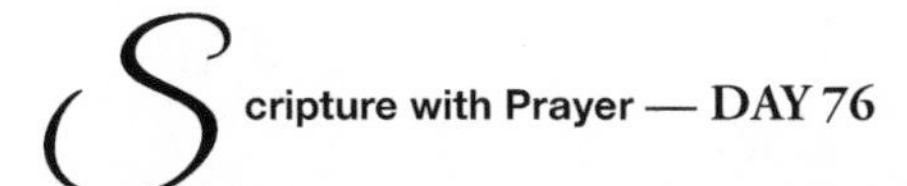

Scripture with Prayer — DAY 76

Do not be anxious then, saying, 'What shall we eat?' or 'What shall we drink?' or 'With what shall we clothe ourselves? -- for your heavenly Father knows that you need all these things. MATTHEW 6:31, 32

PRAYER: Jesus, You personally taught us to faithfully trust in You for all things, including all of our physical needs. Even when You walked the earth, You were more concerned with doing our Father's will than eating food (John 4:34). You created these needs within me, so I ask that You show me how to hand-over control of my strivings (to fulfill all my needs - body, mind, heart) to You, and trust You as my living and loving Shepherd, My King, and My Lord.

Observation / Reflection

___

___

___

___

Application-Reaction / My Next Steps

___

___

___

___

Prayer / Praise / Promises / Gratitude & Thanksgiving

___

___

___

___

Scripture with Prayer — DAY 77

But He said to them, "Why are you so fearful? How is it that you have no faith?" Perfect love casts out fear. Mark 4:40; 1 John 4:18 - NKJ

— Be alert and of sober mind. Your enemy the devil prowls around like a roaring lion looking for someone to devour. Resist him, standing firm in the faith, because you know that the family of believers throughout the world is undergoing the same kind of sufferings. 1 Peter 5:8-9 - NIV

Prayer: Jesus, if living fully in faith and love eliminates anxiety in my life, please show me my next steps toward that goal. Help me maintain alertness of mind and heart for awareness of those spiritual attacks that are inevitable. I give you my spiritual eyes & ears, teach me to see and hear Your guidance.

Observation / Reflection

___

___

___

___

Application-Reaction / My Next Steps

___

___

___

___

Prayer / Praise / Promises / Gratitude & Thanksgiving

___

___

___

___

Scripture with Prayer — DAY 78

O our God, will You not judge them? For we are powerless before this great multitude who are coming against us; nor do we know what to do, but our eyes are on You." —— and he said, "Listen, all Judah and the inhabitants of Jerusalem and King Jehoshaphat: thus says the Lord to you, 'Do not fear or be dismayed because of this great multitude, for the battle is not yours but God's. 2 CHRONICLES 20:12,15 - KJV

PRAYER: I see in this Old Testament record of peril facing Israel, a godly response relevant for me — I should look only to You for help in trouble as opposed to trying to solve problems without You. Help me to rely on You for safety and direction in these situations. In place of fear, I will keep my trust firmly on You!

Observation / Reflection

Application-Reaction / My Next Steps

Prayer / Praise / Promises / Gratitude & Thanksgiving

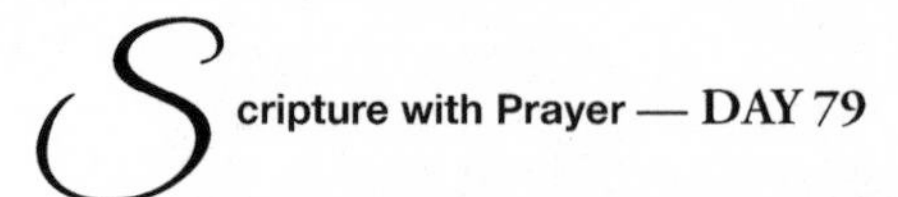

Scripture with Prayer — DAY 79

For I know the thoughts that I think toward you, says the LORD, thoughts of peace and not of evil, to give you a future and a hope.

JEREMIAH 29:11 - NKJ

PRAYER: Lord, thank You that Your thoughts toward me are full of Hope & peace. I know that You have a clear purpose for my life, though it is not fully clear to me yet. You promise that I will find it when I seek, teach me how to hear Your voice. Envelop me with Your Spirit so I may see that purpose, so I may obey and walk-out Your divine will. My greatest hope is that I fulfill what You have ordained for my pilgrimage until the time I see You face to face.

Observation / Reflection

Application-Reaction / My Next Steps

Prayer / Praise / Promises / Gratitude & Thanksgiving

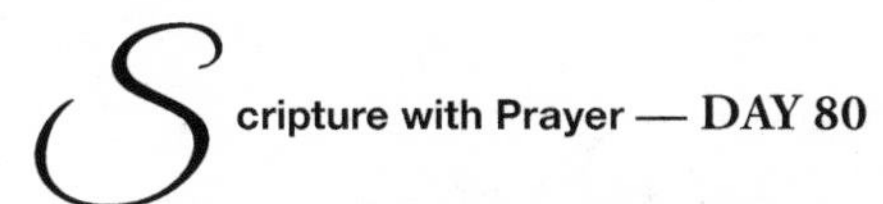

Scripture with Prayer — DAY 80

Are not two sparrows sold for a copper coin? And not one of them falls to the ground apart from your Father's will. But the very hairs of your head are all numbered. Do not fear therefore; you are of more value than many sparrows.
MATTHEW 10:29-31 - NKJ

PRAYER: Father, I can find peace and rest in the faith that, since You created all and You know all, there is a purpose for my trials that I do not immediately understand. I remain steadfast and calm in Your faithfulness and love.

Observation / Reflection

Application-Reaction / My Next Steps

Prayer / Praise / Promises / Gratitude & Thanksgiving

Scripture with Prayer — DAY 81

Whoever dwells in the shelter of the Most High will rest in the shadow of the Almighty. I will say of the Lord, "He is my refuge and my fortress, my God, in whom I trust."He will cover you with his feathers, and under his wings you will find refuge; his faithfulness will be your shield and rampart. You will not fear the terror of night, nor the arrow that flies by day, … For he will command his angels concerning you to guard you in all your ways; they will lift you up in their hands, so that you will not strike your foot against a stone. PSALM 91:1-2,4-5,11-12 - NIV

PRAYER: Thank you for Your protection. You are my refuge and security. I am grateful that You have provided such places for me to hide in my distress, I feel loved and cared for under Your loving wings. Thank You for comforting peace.

Observation / Reflection

___

___

___

___

Application-Reaction / My Next Steps

___

___

___

___

Prayer / Praise / Promises / Gratitude & Thanksgiving

___

___

___

___

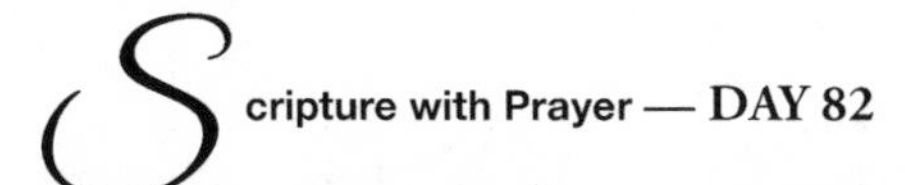

But now in Christ Jesus you who once were far away have been brought near through the blood of Christ. For he himself is our peace. EPHESIANS 2:13-14 NIV
Come unto me, all ye that labour and are heavy laden, and I will give you rest. MATTHEW 11:28 - KJV

PRAYER: Jesus, since you made a way of peace and also invited me to enter on that pathway, I should surely be faithful to obey and enter into Your rest. A humble heart is what you desire, I give you mine today! Open my eyes to both see my labors and burdens clearly so I may lay them down and rest in Your loving arms. My hope is in You my Savior, I praise You with gratitude and thanksgiving.

Observation / Reflection

___

___

___

___

Application-Reaction / My Next Steps

___

___

___

___

Prayer / Praise / Promises / Gratitude & Thanksgiving

___

___

___

___

Scripture with Prayer — DAY 83

Finally, believers, whatever is true, whatever is honorable and worthy of respect, whatever is right and confirmed by God's word, whatever is pure and wholesome, whatever is lovely and brings peace, whatever is admirable and of good repute; if there is any excellence, if there is anything worthy of praise, think continually on these things *[center your mind on them, and implant them in your heart].* ***The things which you have learned and received and heard and seen in me, practice these things*** *[in daily life],* ***and the God*** *[who is the source]* ***of peace and well-being will be with you.***

Philippians 4:8-9 - AMP

Prayer: You have peace. As a believer, it is promised but I haven't been diligent to obey & 'walk in it'! Help me choose Philippians 4 thoughts today!

Observation / Reflection

Application-Reaction / My Next Steps

Prayer / Praise / Promises / Gratitude & Thanksgiving

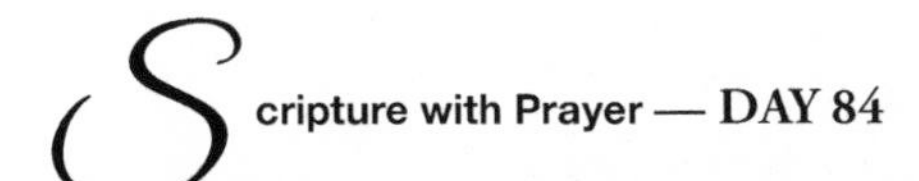

Scripture with Prayer — DAY 84

Now may the Lord of peace Himself continually grant you peace in every circumstance. - peace from Him who is and who was and who is to come. 2

THESSALONIANS 3:16; REVELATIONS1:4 - NAS

PRAYER: Lord, I see that true peace comes from You, and that rule will not change for all eternity. I know that I cannot do anything in my own efforts to acquire the peaceful countenance resulting from Your presence within me, so I ask that You bless and guide my mind and heart, to seek strength and wisdom from You. Teach me to be humble, obedient, and submit to Your leading so I may draw all my needs from You.

Observation / Reflection

____

____

____

____

Application-Reaction / My Next Steps

____

____

____

____

Prayer / Praise / Promises / Gratitude & Thanksgiving

____

____

____

____

Scripture with Prayer — DAY 85

Now no chastening seems to be joyful for the present, but painful; nevertheless, afterward it yields the peaceable fruit of righteousness to those who have been trained by it. —Therefore strengthen the hands which hang down, and the feeble knees, and make straight paths for your feet, so that what is lame may not be dislocated, but rather be healed. Pursue peace with all people, and holiness, without which no one will see the Lord.

HEBREWS 12:11-14 - NKJ

PRAYER: I know that since I am Your child, You will faithfully guide me by all means necessary, and it is for my personal protection & growth. So let me find comfort in these times & cooperate peacefully with the process — to submit all of my life and circumstances to You. Help me be content in all things.

Observation / Reflection

____

____

____

____

Application-Reaction / My Next Steps

____

____

____

____

Prayer / Praise / Promises / Gratitude & Thanksgiving

____

____

____

____

Scripture with Prayer — DAY 86

But the wisdom from above is first pure *[morally and spiritually undefiled],* ***then peace-loving*** *[courteous, considerate],* ***gentle, reasonable*** *[and willing to listen],* ***full of compassion and good fruits. — It is unwavering, without*** *[self-righteous]* ***hypocrisy*** *[and self-serving guile].* ***And the seed whose fruit is righteousness*** *(spiritual maturity)* ***is sown in peace by those who make peace*** *[by actively encouraging goodwill between individuals].* JAMES 3:17-18 - AMP

PRAYER: Lord, help me to seek Your wisdom & walk in a peaceful spirit. To remain in a bond of love, producing Your fruits of goodness for others' sake. Eliminate pride & self-righteousness within me. Help me grow strong in You.

Observation / Reflection

Application-Reaction / My Next Steps

Prayer / Praise / Promises / Gratitude & Thanksgiving

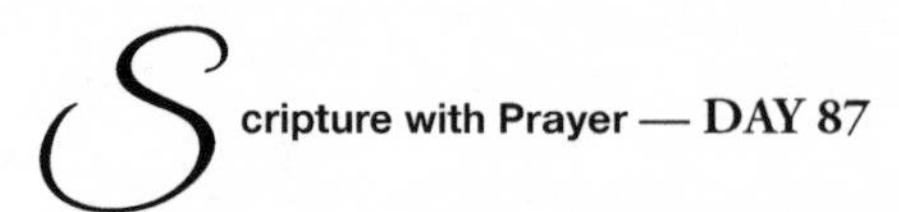

Scripture with Prayer — DAY 87

Aaronic Blessing

The LORD bless you, and keep you; The LORD make His face shine on you, And be gracious to you; The LORD lift up His countenance on you, And give you peace. Numbers 6:24-26 - NKJ

Prayer: Thank You for the blessing of the peace of Your presence! Oh Holy Lord, keep me from offending You in any way as I go about today's tasks. Keep me under the umbrella of Your peace and help me release anything that hinders my steps in Your divine serenity. As I prayerfully 'put on' peaceful shoes every morning, I am learning of You (Ephesians 6:15)— I love You more each day.

Observation / Reflection

____

____

____

____

Application-Reaction / My Next Steps

____

____

____

____

Prayer / Praise / Promises / Gratitude & Thanksgiving

____

____

____

____

Scripture with Prayer — DAY 88

IN GOD'S PRESENCE IS THE FULLNESS OF LOVE AND PEACE :

There is no fear in love *[dread does not exist],* ***but full-grown*** *(complete, perfect)* ***love turns fear out of doors and expels every trace of terror! For fear brings with it the thought of punishment, and*** *[so]* ***he who is afraid has not reached the full maturity of love*** *[is not yet grown into love's complete perfection]*·

1 JOHN 4:18 AMP

PRAYER: Dear Heavenly Father, I love being in Your presence where I feel perfect peace. Yet, at times I am consumed by worry & fear. When that happens, please come and comfort me with Your Holy Spirit. Help me stay close to you always. Reveal to me anything that inhibits me from remaining fully under Your umbrella of love, guide me in Your path of safety, provision, rest & contentment.

Observation / Reflection

____
____
____
____

Application-Reaction / My Next Steps

____
____
____
____

Prayer / Praise / Promises / Gratitude & Thanksgiving

____
____
____
____

Scripture with Prayer — DAY 89

Away with you, Satan! For it is written, 'You shall worship the LORD your God, and Him only you shall serve.' Then the devil left Him, and behold, angels came and ministered to Him. - Resist the devil, and he will flee from you.

MATTHEW 4:10, JAMES 4:7 - NKJ

PRAYER: Jesus, thank You for showing how to fend off Satan's attacks. When I am under-fire, bring to my mind Your Word, and it will send him away. Provide discernment so I clearly see these attacks, and strength so I can quickly fight off temptations or negative emotions. By Your Spirit, minister peace deep within me.

Observation / Reflection

____

____

____

____

Application-Reaction / My Next Steps

____

____

____

____

Prayer / Praise / Promises / Gratitude & Thanksgiving

____

____

____

____

Scripture with Prayer — DAY 90

But Jesus immediately said to them: "Take courage! It is I. Don't be afraid." MATTHEW 14:27

Your life is hidden with Christ in God. COLOSSIANS 3:3 NIV
He makes me to lie down in green pastures; He leads me beside the still waters. He restores my soul. PSALM 23:2-3 - NKJ

PRAYER: Jesus, I love Your Word — it brings peace to my spirit knowing my life is hidden in You! Oh what comfort! As my Shepherd I can trust fully that You will guide me in all safety, to rest in Your shadow. In Your care, I don't have to look for things to worry about. Help me walk-out these promises today in faith!

Observation / Reflection

___

___

___

___

Application-Reaction / My Next Steps

___

___

___

___

Prayer / Praise / Promises / Gratitude & Thanksgiving

___

___

___

___

NOTES

Made in the USA
San Bernardino, CA
04 December 2018